My S
The Bad and the Ugly
preparation for my destiny

By Tiffany Anderson

Motivational Speaker and Author

Dedication

The Bible tells us in Matthew 22:14 "that many are called but few are chosen." It would be many years later that I could honestly stand up boldly and say, "Thank you, Jesus!" for choosing me. The idea that we are chosen to do good is great but it's another thing to be chosen to endure such pain in the hopes that one day you would run back and tell someone else how Amazing God is.

For example, in the story when Jesus healed the ten lepers in Luke 17:11-19, the fact that only one came back to say thank you still amazes me. But today we live in a world where people are okay as long as you don't stand boldly with your story on how amazing God has been. We are okay, as long as we don't talk about certain things, especially in the African American communities.

So, unlike the other nine lepers, I want to first give a standing ovation, a round of applause, and complete utter gratitude to God, Jesus, and the Holy Spirit. I am thankful for everything I had to endure to get me to this place that I never imagined for myself.

I want to thank my family, friends and even my enemies for whatever role you played to get me to this place. Family, I love you.

To my village, I love you beyond measure.

Last but not least, I want to thank my beautiful daughters Jia Taylor and Tiana Dai for blessing me with the crown of being called "Mother." To my first born Jia, I thank you for coming into my life, right on time, and forever changing my life. You are truly a gift from God and I will always love you mostest. You remind me so much of how I used to be, and I hope you love the God you see in your mommy. You are so beautiful, brilliant, smart and important. The sky is the limit. Keep God first, seek his face and all these things will be added.

To my last one, the real Princess Tiana, the wise one! Girl, to say you are your own person is an under-statement. I recall people saying, "You know, she may not be like Jia," and boy, were they right! You came out and took complete ownership of your own identity and destiny, never settling for just being Jia's little sister. You represent where I am now and where God is taking me, so smart but so compassionate and caring. I love you mostest.

I thank God for the gift of life and to give life. I pray that this book helps but also provides healing that God desperately desires so that you can be all that he has called and created each of us to be!

Table of Contents

Foreword

Have you ever met a young woman who was extremely wise beyond her years? Have you ever met a young woman whose life story just blew you away? Well, fasten your seat belts because you're in for the ride of your life.

Tiffany was one of the youngest women who spoke at the 2015 Powerful Journey Women's Conference. There wasn't a dry eye in the building as hundreds of women heard her heroic life story. Lives were impacted, influenced and changed for the better. That's her mission, which has become her passion and purpose.

Many young women who have experienced half of what Tiffany has experienced would be bitter and mad with the world. But Tiffany is using what happened to her as a platform to help as many women and girls as possible. She's teaching valuable life lessons learned in hopes of saving others from a life of turmoil.
Tiffany's story is evidence that if you trust God, persevere and don't ever give up, you can become the overcomer that you were created to become.
To God be the glory for the many lives that will be changed because His daughter, Tiffany didn't sit on her story.

Phyllis Jenkins, CPC |Author| Speaker
phyllisjenkins.com
Powerful Journey Speakers Platform, Founder power of God upon one who deeply desires to please Him.

Preface

"Why so much suffering and pain so young," I asked God at twenty-one years old?

Or, "How many times have I written this book?" is the real question.

I started writing this book when I was about ten years old. During this time of complete and utter turmoil, I was full of all kind of hurt and hatred. My mom had gone to prison the year before. Although one would have thought this would have been a happy ending to the hell we had endured, for me it was only the beginning. Life had been filled with so much pain at such an early age that I grew to expect it, get through it, and eventually I grew numb to it. This was a process that I would continue well into my adult life.

Over the years, as I have gained a better understanding of God's love for us. I have rewritten the book it seemed with each stage of my life. So although my daughters share the same parents, they actually have been raised by two different moms. I say this because I was in two different stages in my life with each birth, therefore a completely different parent. The foundation is the same but the mind, state, and the heart are completely different. So when I initially wrote the book it was to expose and let the world know that I had an awful mom and she inflicted hell into my life for the first nine years of it. It also spoke of the failure of society, CPS, and police to rescue me from the pits of hell. Lastly, it spoke of the audacity of the family and church to do absolutely nothing but add fury to the fire. The funny thing about this is that no one knew who the heck I was, so who would that actually benefit? I have replayed this over and over in my mind, and the fact is it would have served no purpose at that time.

With each stage or phase the book grew softer and softer and less dark and ugly. The purpose of the book in those years really had no benefit because it satisfied the devil and what he wants us as children of God to see and feel in the midst of our trials and tribulations. In all reality although they might hurt--and boy, did it hurt— but in my case hurting didn't really matter because no one saw that I was fit to be freed from this pain. No matter where I turned, I felt that matters simply got worse or that they felt I had gotten what I deserved. I couldn't trust anyone, and that is how I began to live my life and cope. Who's going to care? What did your mom do? What did your family do? Who the heck is your daddy? Where is he? What did the police and CPS do? Okay, so it's just you. It would take more than twenty-five years, in the midst of a divorce, and at one of the lowest times in my life when I felt alone the most. But at this time I am spiritually ready to rewrite this book for the last time and for the complete benefit of God's GLORY.

When you begin to read this, you might think I am out of my mind. Hopefully by the end of it, you will agree that, no matter what, God is amazing. This book is open, honest and completely transparent, so I hope you are ready. But what I don't want you to feel by reading this book is sympathy or pity for me. Perhaps I wish you a reality check to be more mindful of how you treat innocent children who may still be going through the things God delivered me from. Be more compassionate and loving throughout the year–not because of a season—and know that God is good. Please join me as I share with you my times of severe mental, verbal, physical and sexual abuse that extends from the age of two years old. Pain has followed me most of my life with no major counseling, on my own and ostracized by loved ones and others only to learn I had been chosen to endure for such a time as this!

Satan wants us to be distracted by our obstacles, trials and tribulations. He wants us to be blind to God's goodness in the midst of our situations. In all reality, this is my book from the best of my memory and through my eyes of hurt and pain.

I realize we are human and all make mistakes. Some things happen out of our own poor choices, while, other things happen before you are old enough to make your own choices. None-the-less, God is still good in what appears to be your mess. He specializes in house cleaning!

The message is simple, "Until you can learn to thank and praise God in the midst of the good, the bad and the ugly, you are just living, not thriving!"

The Bible says in Ephesians 3:20, "Now unto him that is able to do exceeding abundantly above all that we ask or think, according to the power that works in us." And also Philippians 1:6: "...being confident of this that he who began a good work in you will carry it on to completion until the day of Christ Jesus. These are constant reminders to me that he will start what he finished in you and that he can exceed what we ask or think!

He has already promised in his word that he will never leave nor forsake us. I have spent most of my life angry and mad at the world. I focused so much on the bad childhood I had that I couldn't find the good or God in it. But I hope you will realize in the midst of whatever you are going through, God is still good. He can turn it around for your good, if you will allow him to. Don't spend the rest of your life giving the devil victory. Instead, I encourage you to start thanking and praising God right now for the fact that you are still here.

Introduction

"OUT......OUT.....OUT OF MY HOUSE," I screamed and pointed towards the door!

I had never fathomed that I would have what one would consider a "weak girl" moment, but I did!

But I had enough, I yelled and screamed, threw his things out of my house and fussed sounding like Rosie Perez with each sentence!

I recalled the day God told me I would marry him, and I remember telling God, "No, I will not!" We hadn't spoken for years, and he had been incarcerated. But God began to show me that I was no better than him in his eyes. The past few years, with him in my home and in my life reminded me of an all too familiar nightmare I experienced a greater part of my life and childhood. One that was filled with a lack of peace, joy and filled with pure utter CHAOS! I couldn't even sleep at night in my home, and I vowed as a child I would never allow anyone to steal my joy, peace and a night's rest.

Somehow, he had successfully sucked what life, peace and joy I had right out of my body. I recalled situations throughout the marriage and thought how you got to this place. He was a very kind and gentle man, but his issues with addictions proved to be much more than I could handle. I thought about all I had worked hard for as a single mother and felt I was in a good place to help someone else.

I always found myself trying to help everyone but myself. I had a word of advice, a prayer, an extra dollar, baby-sitting, loans and have even provided room and board for a handful of family members in need. While I was a single mother myself, in fact, most of my child's life, yet I always found myself putting my needs, our needs at the bottom. It seemed like once people got what they wanted, needed or had gotten to a better place they were on to either talk about you or on with their own lives. This vicious cycle of behavior, I learned, was a result of all I had gone through and overcome. It made me more compassionate and empathetic than most. But at the same time, the abuse and neglect I had endured as a child became something that I continued even against myself well into my adult life.

Now, the next few weeks and months and year would prove to be some of the hardest. I knew this because after the job loss, the loss of everything I worked hard for, then the marriage failing, there were no family or friends to turn to. I was hurt and disappointed in myself for letting this happen. You have no idea how it was to live a life where being successful was not a part of it. I have been fighting my whole life to avoid becoming a statistic. Once again, nothing worked out good for me. As my Pastor says now, if it wasn't for bad luck, many of us wouldn't know what luck was! Months before this breaking point, I had begun lying in the floor prostrate each night, in tears asking God what did he want from me? I was so frustrated but I was tired and I asked him boldly, "WHAT do you want from me?"

"You got my attention. There is no one to turn to. Now what do you want from me?" I began to ask him to deal with me, show me myself and more importantly those in my life. I turned away from the microscope and asked for a mirror to show me Tiffany.

You know that saying, "Be careful what you ask for!" Whoa, there is so much truth to this; I had waged war with the wrong one. But he knew I could handle it, why my entire childhood had prepared me for it! Then over the next year he began to manifest himself in my life like never before. He showed up in my dreams.

At one point I felt like "Scrooge." He began to take me back to my childhood, back to specific encounters with people and slowly began to answer all the questions I had waged against him all at once. He showed me things and people so clearly, but because I was not prepared to receive it, they all blew up in my face.

Because the truth was more than I could handle, most of those relationships ended abruptly for a time. I say this, when people tell you something about someone, listen; but when God shows you something believe him! So although the marriage failed, I lost everything, I was alone and endured some of the hardest times as the sole provider of my girls, I overcame all these difficulties.

Ultimately, I realized that I was an addict as well, and it took the marriage and divorce to bring peace that I have been unknowingly seeking since I was a child. I became so numb to pain at such an early age that I not only began to inflict pain on myself, but I allowed it from people around me, and I began to thrive off of it. I was a pain addict and it would take nearly twenty-five years before I would realize and take ownership of this very thing.

I pray that you receive all that you need through God in me as I share on the following pages some of the most hurtful times in my life but how God showed me it was indeed preparation for my destiny. I have learned that "Every lesson has a blessing!" But you have to learn the lesson and pass the test.

1

Ouch, that hurt!

Will this ever end and is all that life has to offer me was ALL I could think about as a child? Or was it, "Here we go again?" Who knows honestly? I don't recall.

I don't remember coloring, having fun or playing with dolls ever during this time. Even as I sit here now, I cannot think of a pleasant or happy time, but one thing I do see is PAIN, everything HURT. The pain was so real in my life, it was all I knew and felt. Eventually, I grew numb by the time I turned nine years old. Can you imagine? Look around do you have or know of a nine year old, take a good look at him or her. Then as you read this book whether you are a teen, adult, or someone older, contemplating whether or not anything in the Bible is authentic; I hope that through my story you will grasp he is alive, he is good, he was there, and he loves you.

I am from a small town in Oklahoma, and there is not much I remember about this place before nine years old. Matter of a fact, there is hardly anything I remember outside of pain. The first couple of years of my life I don't even remember, and it would be years before I would find out much about this time even though I do not remember.

I realized at some point that I had never seen a picture of myself before nine years old. For me, it was confirmation of what I had felt and experienced a greater part of my life. I had always felt different, mistreated, like the black sheep and the doormat of the family. So maybe it was then that I realized I was so hated that no one even wanted evidence of my mere existence.

I went from house to house and photo album to photo album and could not find one. I began to inquire and no one knew, but they referred me to my grandma. I went to her, and she told me to go ask Tootsie. Tootsie was one of my grand-mother's best friends. I cannot recall if she was one that grew up as friends or over the years they became friends. Nonetheless, I went to see Tootsie and to my surprise, there were baby pictures of me all the way up until I was maybe two years old. She began to share stories and although I tried I just could not remember those times at all.

But one thing that did come from it is that I realized a few things. At one point I was pretty, I had a head full of hair, and someone loved me. She told me that after months of seeing me being severely neglected and left at home by myself as a newborn, she asked my mom if she could just take care of me. My mom allowed her to take me. She told me during this time we lived in Houston for a little while and also that my mom moved to another part of Oklahoma.

Somewhere along the way, I was kidnapped or taken away from her to get more money from the government. Whatever the reason, I was just happy to see a happy kid at some point although I have no memories of this time. But I thank her for trying to help me but also for filling a void in my life.

Although I cannot recall professional pictures, it was just strange sitting here looking at pictures of me in this lady's house, in her album, yet I don't even remember her. Furthermore, she is not a blood relative which made it even stranger. She only allowed me to take four pictures from her album, and I treasured them forever, yet I cannot find them to this day.

Tootsie has since then passed away. Sadly, there is no evidence of any of my baby pictures retrieved or kept. But this allowed me to see just how bad my life had gotten between my time with Tootsie and mom's imprisonment.

Where do I start?

Well, I think back and recall when I first remember being sexually molested. I had to have been from two to four years old, as I was not old enough to go to school. I then recall it going through my time going to school half a day and then once school started.

I cannot only see these things in my dreams; I was a little black girl who was skinny, ugly with nappy hair and freckles. How do I get stuck with all the freckles and nappy hair? I would recall that my offender never allowed me to go outside or play with my sisters. He kept me inside and had his way with me.

Of course, I didn't know that anything was wrong with this. I was just a little girl but it hurt like everything else in my life, so I just thought this was life and how it was supposed to be.

Then there is this constant physical and verbal abuse; I recall always getting butt naked beatings with extension cords. I could see my white t-shirt and panties on the couch and I really wanted just to put on maybe twenty pairs of jeans to prevent the constant pain and agony I always felt. That white t-shirt and panties on the couch was always an indication that somebody was about to get into big trouble, but somehow this was normal so I'm unsure if anybody really processed the extent of the pain.

I remember the beating being so hateful because it could go from beatings that left me numb, to being stomped in the same setting or slung all over the floor.

I think the picture on the cover of this book describes my view of the world which started as a child, from the ground up, but always at someone's feet. Even once God revealed to me many years later his love for me and his value and purpose in my life but every life. I could not fully grasp this idea or concept from my view of life always at the bottom of the totem pole. My pastor always says, "If it wasn't for bad luck, I wouldn't have any luck at all!"

I still see my sisters going into the room scheming and plotting against me so that I could get their beatings. I felt they had probably grown tired of their share of pains. Eventually, I came along and they decided since mama hated me most, I would be their scape goat.

Especially, if they did something that they knew would make mama upset, they would team up and decide that I did it! Sadly, this feeling didn't end here; I think for the most of my life I have always felt not only ostracized by my family but my sisters as well.
The bruises would be so bad that I would wear winter clothes in the summer to hide the bruises, but that often didn't work. To this day, I hate to be hot, and I would get nonstop headaches in my childhood. It was from the physical abuse and my hair being ripped from my head. I also threw up a lot and I knew once I complained my

teachers would take me out of class. They would attempt to change my clothes and then they would discover the bruises once again.

So not only was this numbing pain that I developed as a young child to build up the tolerance to withstand the beatings, the sexual molestation and now the humiliation. The humiliation would involve them removing my clothes and taking a lot of pictures, as I stood in my panties. I guess this would be their evidence to call the police again and have me taken away from my mother.

I remember those rides in the police car. I would always have a little change in my pocket, begging the officer to take me to the store so I could spend it. But of course this was serious and therefore they would never make the stop. They would take me straight to this group home or something like a waiting home before foster care, I think. I didn't see the purpose of this place; for example, in my case, a severely abused and battered child out of one crazy environment to another. Then, I would be placed amongst kids that had all sorts of issues, into this one environment without getting to the root of any problem. But more so, providing a holding place for these kids until something could be done.

So here I am in this group home facility and I am seeing kids come and go, along with being bullied as well because of my physical condition. I often cried, threw up and prayed that the pain in my head and body would stop. It seemed constant in this place to no avail.

Then, I thought because no one would pick me I would be given back to my mother, to go basically back to the same life as before. I thought in my head now, what was the point of taking me, especially, if you were just going to give me back to my mom?

But I see how people treat people differently because of the physical appearance when in all actuality you had no idea of the hell they may have to endure in one day. I thought about how awful that felt, and how these types of pains are life lasting. Yes, I will discuss several things that I still do or refuse to do to this day because of my past. I hope that parents will understand that everything you do or expose your children to becomes a part of who you are training them to be.

This was my life day in and day out; I thought this was normal but painful.

I can recall sitting at the dinner table all day after being forced to eat a plate of food that most adults could not consume. If you could not eat all the food you sat there all day. So, I remember many times sitting there all day. I couldn't imagine making my children sit at the table all day if they could not eat all the food on their plate. But I confess to this day there are still certain foods I cannot eat to this day. I cannot say if it's a mental block or preference but I just don't.

Then there were these long stints of being locked in closets without being fed for periods of time. Again, you don't really understand the long term effects this has on innocent children.

I recall one time that was very specific because I would lie with my face as close to the crack between the floor and the door. I could see light and my family going on as if I didn't exist.

But there was the time I was let out just in time to attend some sort of carnival near our apartment complex. I can remember just being hungry, and so the first opportunity I got, I entered a pie eating contest. The crazy thing is that I was the only child and these adults must have thought, Now what does this little girl think she is about to do?

Needless to say, I won the contest and ironically some time later, my little face consuming this pie was plastered all over the billboards on the streets of Tulsa, Oklahoma. It was for the "Feed the Hungry Children Network!" I am not certain how all of that worked back in the day, but I later learned that they didn't have the right to take the picture of me and that my mom may have gotten a financial settlement as a result. The fact that they took this picture of a small kid consuming this pie but no one thought to help her is beyond me.

My mom was crazy is all I can say at this point. I thought on the times she got ready to get us and it could be anywhere if the family were there, they got a ghost. I felt that everyone in our family was afraid of her or just didn't want to deal with the drama. I remember moments of "Okay, it's time for us to go" when she would go on a rampage. So I look back thinking how sad it is for kids to be treated this way and no one helps them.

I still remember us lying in bed singing this song we had made up, "I'm hungry!" It was a song that we would sing when our mom would send us to bed without eating or would be gone all day with no food. We would be too afraid to get out of the bed but we would sing.

It's a funny thought now, but in that moment being hungry one minute and then being stuffed like a pig the next was just crazy!

I remember lots of schools, different teachers, but not one face or image of a friend that I can remember before "Doomsday!" I can remember times that my mom would get into it with men she was dating and somehow we would be caught in the middle. We would be on the run in the middle of the night, terrified as if our lives were in danger. Heck, maybe it was. I don't know or I'm unsure if I could comprehend that at the time. I saw, heard, and felt things that no child my age or any of us should have experienced for many years.

I remember the time I had an allergic reaction to a tetanus shot. It left me with a leg that wouldn't allow me to move for days. I could only sit in the Indian style seated position. So my mom made me stay home by myself until I could walk again. I know I sat up in this room for days, kind of waiting for my siblings to come home. Then I wouldn't feel alone. I had no idea this type of abuse and neglect would follow me well into my adult life.

There was a church bus that came through the apartments we lived in. I don't know that I really understood church or its purpose at that time. I just knew that at church and school things were different. People were nice and we were in a pain free zone! But to say, I remember specific situations or encounters during this time, it's all a blur.

I cannot even say that I prayed because I would hope no God above would surely witness the hell we endured and allow us to remain there! Honestly, I can say anywhere my Mom went was not was a fun place, at least not from what I can remember. I think she loved us as best as she knew love to be.

These situations were some of the situations that were used to haunt me during my early childhood. My family used this to taunt and tease me for years to come. For me, it served as a constant reminder that you were lower than the scum of the earth, you had no value, and you certainly weren't going to amount to anything.

I didn't love myself, and why would I? Love had no love for me. I looked around a year or so ago and realized I didn't close doors in my home. This is because I was locked in closets as a child. Most of the things I do or don't do now are because of the horrible things I endured.

You're crazy if you think that people can just get over their past or that it doesn't have an impact on their lives forever. I have already mentioned there are still foods I don't eat to this day. I don't trust many people, and I often keep people at a distance, so when they do hurt you it will not hurt as bad. This is just a small reminder that it can take years or a lifetime to heal from these wounds many years later.

At this point, I had grown numb to life and all the pains that come with it. I sit here trying to think of a smile, laughter, fun, a particular friend, a teacher, a school any memory before the age of nine that was good, and unfortunately there were none. The memories were awful and ouch, it hurt!

2

Doomsday

Bam...Bam...Bam....was the sound we heard, which
turned into a profuse beating on the front door!
I could imagine we were just young kids so we were
probably terrified to open the door. You know during
those days you were told not to answer the door when
your parents were not home or else. Heck, it really
didn't matter for me because "or else" was the story of
my life. But there came this day when the life we knew
would soon end. This knock on the door changed us for
the rest of our lives.

I don't remember anything that happened on this
particular day other than being awakened early that
morning, if that makes sense. So that means it was too
late for children to be left home but yet too early for us
to be up getting into trouble. I just remember it was

chaotic because the police and my aunt had come to get us to advise that our Mom would not be coming home. It was way too much to process or even understand in that moment. I knew our lives would forever be changed. I loved my Mom because she was all we had known up until this point. But how can you love anyone else when you had not been taught or shown it?

My mom went to prison for taking someone's life, and there were so many rumors surrounding this case that I am unsure I know the truth to this very day. I do know that at the time that she was locked up in prison she was pregnant with my youngest brother. He was born a few months after her prison sentence, and he came home to my aunt. She is still his other mother to this day.

I cannot imagine how my mom may have felt giving birth to a child and being forced to see him go. But at the same time my brother would be confused for the rest of his childhood. He wouldn't know who the heck his real mother was, and that was just the beginning. If I am not mistaken, I believe a year or so later my aunt gave birth to her last child, her youngest daughter. So we had two babies or toddlers in the home.

The babies were much too young to understand all that was going on. But they made us forget about all our problems, that's for certain. Who wouldn't? Babies are beautiful, they smell good and they just make you happy!

I just thought maybe God had enough of all the evil and hateful things she had done and needed to remove her from society. I look back and I think that prison, in an effort to change her life, ultimately saved our lives. Or would it? Society doesn't realize that often times when a parent or person receives a prison sentence, unfortunately, so do their children. Although we committed no crime as her children, we did the time too.

The life we had known ended, but a new chapter began. Now, you have a bunch of beat down and battered children that needed more help than we got and more love than any one person could give. In a sense, although my physical situation changed, my spirit was ruined.

Even though it seemed that loving this woman hurt, maybe my existence was a reminder of something or someone she wanted to forget, nonetheless, I loved her. Or did I? In the days and weeks to come, life had changed, and it was so different I could not understand.

But there were things I noticed, and it was almost instantly. The pain that I had known before no longer existed. Before this time, I didn't even know that constant pain was not normal, and how I was treated was wrong.

There was a lot of confusion initially. I thought for days and weeks that this was not how I was supposed to be treated all this time. I was left angry, bitter, cold, and hateful. I hated my Mom, I hated myself, and I hated life and everything it had offered me up until this point.

I think I had grown addicted to this pain, and now that it was gone I didn't know how to live or respond to this new life. One would think that you would be relieved that your mom was now taken away because this hateful life of pain was now coming to an end.

Yet somehow I felt that this left me worse off because there was so much I didn't understand. Our family was so sick with generational curses that consistently allowed innocent children to be abused because they were too afraid to get involved.

I heard that the deceased man's family had made threats against our family and Mom's kids. But in the midst of all the chaos I cannot confirm that. I do know that this day forever changed the rest of our lives, and I cannot say for the better.

I know that I had grown addicted to pain. I expected and looked for it, so when it stopped cold turkey out of nowhere, I didn't know how to process the abrupt change. I was used to crying myself to sleep, going numb in the midst of a beating, never having fun or laughing much, and then it ended!
With this came all sorts of emotions that I didn't know how to process or where to turn to get help. Now, I realized everything I had gone through was wrong.

How was I supposed to trust anyone? Who could you trust when everyone you should trust, let you down? One day I was the ugly, beat down, freckled face and nappy- headed little girl, and the next day I was free. It was different, and it was externally pain free. But I hated the world and everything in it. My heart grew smart; it built a wall around it to protect me from being hurt any longer.

Now, we were in this beautiful home with my aunt. They had a good life and here we come, all these kids that needed help. I felt that our presence turned their world inside out. They lived in a nice neighborhood on the north side. They had a nice house, yard, friends, and their own rooms. Then in the blink of an eye we are all up in their personal space. Heck, I know they didn't like it, but neither did I.

My mom had one request, and that was that all of her children stayed together. I say this all the time; we are only as good as we were raised to be. My aunt was a young adult herself with her own kids and life. I look back and think there is no way I would take in all those darn kids. Especially for someone who had been so evil.

Sometimes we as adults make decisions for children that we think are best for us instead of what's best for them. We needed so much love and help that a single parent home with someone so young was not the best option. Now, that was my opinion as I look back on the situation. I don't want anyone to think we didn't appreciate what my aunt did, but as a parent sometimes what's best for you is not what's best for your children or your home.

This arrangement stirred up our cousins' lives and what they knew to be normal, and I don't blame them for being mad at us, their mom or the entire situation. I was angry, and it had nothing to do with them. I had experienced things kids our age just shouldn't have had to. We were all too young to comprehend the severity of our situations. Or maybe too young to understand how good God was. Better yet, at that time I was thinking, who or where was God?

But when your life is crazy who has time to stop and think about all that? I hated myself more during this time. I would hurt myself because pain was the drug I needed and had missed. I could see myself beating my head on the pillow and shaking my leg to rock myself to sleep at night. I believe this was a beat and rock cope method I had learned over all those years of abuse.

I remember I used to cut, torture and beat myself up in a manner to cause pain I had gotten used to. I know it was during this time that I went from being the bullied to becoming the bully. My emotions were all over the place. My aunt tried to get us counseling.

There was one session that I would never forget and I know that it made me shut down completely. The counselor was an older Caucasian female that gave me a little white Bible with a gold cross as the zipper. I was so excited and felt so special, but once she began to speak, I realized I could not trust her either. My own family didn't understand me or my situation. Now, to have someone who doesn't look like me to tell me that it was okay for me to grow up and be just like everything that happened to me just didn't make sense. I might be ugly, battered and bruised, but I thought I was pretty smart.

But to hear her speak, although it motivated me, it also made me go back into my little shell and never open up again to anyone else. I am not what happened to me and to tell a child that because of their past you can only be as good as life had been to you, was absurd.

I stated things should have gotten better because my mom was gone, but clearly it did not. I was left so angry, cold, bitter and confused. I had become such a bad child. But there was this evangelist at my uncle's church who would put me in a circle and pray those demons up out of me.

When I look back, I cannot say that I didn't have demons, but I think I was more misunderstood. And no one had answers for the confusion or the pain I felt. You are expected to go on with a normal life. Yet, you don't even know what normal looks or feels like. How could I possibly do that?

I had never been shown or given love yet; I should love, smile and be happy. Better yet, get over it! How? Why? Life had not been good to me; my nerves were so bad, and I had no peace of mind. I couldn't even sleep at night, my hair wouldn't grow, and my head wouldn't stop hurting. *Geez.*

I thought I intentionally got into trouble so that I could feel the pain I had always known. I would bully kids for their lunch money and stole from anyone I could. I hated myself and was angered easily by those around me. People tried or wanted to love me, and I didn't understand that language or that feeling. So, I did everything to get attention, love or that feeling of pain I had grown to love.

I felt that I was addicted to pain and just as most addicts have withdrawals in rehab, I was an innocent child suffering from abuse withdrawals. I had been treated like a slave a greater part of my life and then suddenly it ended.

Now, we are with my aunt, and I watched as her kids changed. I had a cousin that was close in age to me, and I admit I probably took a lot of my anger out on her. They used to say we looked alike and would dress us like twins. I couldn't understand it, still don't. She was pretty and I was not. She tried to show me love and be nice, but heck, I couldn't understand why she liked me and wanted to be around.

I was so conflicted at this time because so much had happened I couldn't understand. So, going to counseling ceased because it didn't help me and I often got in trouble more than everyone else. I would even get in trouble if I snuck out and ate during the middle of the night. Heck, I felt like a freed slave, can you imagine that? I could eat, play, and laugh, but I was so troubled and confused.

I loved making mud pies, playing hide and seek, climbing trees, building treehouses, skating, going swimming and just being a child. My aunt had a friend who lived next door, and she was really nice. Their kids were close in age and had become really good friends over the years. I liked to go over there to play but had no idea about sharing or anything like that. But she had dogs, and I was extremely terrified of dogs and everyone knew it. I think she thought by forcing me to deal with the dogs, my fear of them would go away.

Eventually, that life that we had grown accustomed to would soon change. I can imagine that with this extra load of six or seven children in addition to her own children changed life drastically for my aunt. We had to move from the nice north side to the wretched southside, and that is what I meant. Although I vaguely remember things about the first house, I know we lived there for a little while. But it was nothing like the house my aunt and her children had grown up in for years!

I still don't understand why no one else in our family would assist my aunt with all my mom's six or seven kids. My mom had only requested that all of her children remained together. I commend my aunt on all she did, but there is no way I would have done it. I mean, she could have had us for the rest of our young lives. My mom had received a thirty year prison sentence. But my aunt's step sister did try to help as best she could.

I got to live with her for a short time, and it's funny how I think she still looks at me strange even to this day. I don't blame my family, but it doesn't change the facts and how I felt. I had suffered the most, and yet I got the least amount of help, love and support. Everyone just written me off as bad, a liar, a thief, but no one really took the time or invested in getting to the root of the problems. You cannot take a child who had suffered the way I did and expect her to adjust with ease. Looking back, I know I desperately needed something that my family was unable to give and uneducated enough to do for my siblings or myself.

There came a time when we were assigned families or adult mentors to help from my uncle's church, I assumed to assist my aunt since no one else wanted to assist with our situation. Sadly, I see how the ones that needed the most help got stuck with the most unreliable families. Yet the ones that needed the least got the better families in my opinion. For example, two of my siblings still have those families as a part of their life to this day. I was assigned a single man to mentor me.

I had been severely sexually and physically abused, and it didn't make sense to give me a male mentor like that. Maybe they didn't care or just didn't think about it. I don't remember spending much time with him, but I think he ended up passing on a year later, and I had to get a new mentor.

I ended up getting a single woman as a mentor after that. I do have fond memories of being with her, going to her house, going to the store and being at family functions at her house with her. I don't know what happened to her, but she had a nice house and I liked her a lot. I kind of enjoyed being somewhere and getting all the attention. But I said all this to say, I felt I needed a man and woman, a family to support and help me along the way.

I think about all the fun times I had at my uncle's church when I got to do a lot of fun things in the summer and on breaks. We witnessed a lot of fun things with our church for the kids. We were so active; we acted, stepped, rapped, sang and I am sure we faked the Holy Spirit from time to time. Our youth choir was amazing, and we were on fire for Christ. I grew to love the peace I felt when I sang for Jesus and was in his presence. We traveled many places with our youth choir. My aunt told me recently that we were personally invited to come perform in all those places.

That same evangelist who prayed for me would always request that I sing the song "I don't want no peanut butter and jelly!" We still laugh at this song today. I told the story and sang it the same way each time, nothing more and nothing less. I think she requested it so that maybe in time it would transform my heart, mind, and soul. I hated to be in front of people, but I always managed to make it through and never forgot one verse of that story or song! Who knows, but it has been one of the few songs we never forgot.

Christmas and Thanksgiving were always special times of the year for me. They always were and always will be. Have you ever noticed how nice people are during that season of the year? Ironically, it didn't matter who our mom was or that she was in prison because people wanted to be seen as caring and giving during this season. Since our mom was in prison, we got help from Angel Tree and churches for Christmas. How else would us nine to eleven kids have a nice Christmas, much less any Christmas?

Nonetheless, I think the food, the family and the way people looked at us during this season was just different. I wish the spirit of Thanksgiving and Christmas would last all year long. Even to this day, this time of the year is still my favorite. The question remains in my head today, Why aren't people nice like this all year round? Some questions may never get answered!

I have countless good memories of being with my aunt who I thank God for daily. She gave up her life and those of her children all for a simple request from her sister. I can say that although I benefited from this time with her, there were still so many hurts and pains that I had grown numb to at such a young age that no one could help or understand me. The enemy was able to use my unresolved hurts and pains from my past to hinder me a greater part of my life. The enemy wants you to stay in a place; society is used to you being in that space, and yet God is trying to free you from this very place.

Does it mean that the dark days were behind? No, things were just better! Yet, I still felt lost!

3

Sue's Kid

I know you are wondering exactly what does this mean. Well, later in my adult years an author and speaker asked me what my name was as she began to autograph her book I purchased. I replied, "It's just Tiffany, you know it's even spelled simply Tiffany! T-i-f-f-a-n-y, no –i, -ie, -ii, nothing fancy just Tiffany! She gave me her number and email, and she said, "Find out what your name means and get back to me via email or telephone!" She said, "Every time someone speaks your name that is what they are speaking on you." So, I did my research and was surprised at what I learned:

Origin: Greek
Quick Meaning: Appearance of a God
Number of letters: 7, those 7 letters total to 36
Gender: Girl
Latin: Female Variant of Theophania

Greek: Female Gods incarnate.
Tiffany is a common female name. It has originated
from the Greek word Theophania. Tiffany is also used
as the shortened form of Theophana or Theophania.
This name is used in Europe as well as USA. ***This
name also means manifestation of God.***

I was completely blown away at all that I had found in
researching my own name. When I emailed and called
her regarding the meaning of my name, she reminded
me not to ever forget what my name meant.

I just began to reflect on my past and all I had seen and
survived. I am not saying that I am Jesus, nor am I close
to him in any comparison. But to realize that some
things you endure in this life may not be for you but for
the benefit of others. God is amazing because he knows
how much we can bear. I think about how I prayed to
God about what to name my girls, but I never gave any
thought to the importance of your name. When I grew
up it was irrelevant, especially after my Mom went to
prison.

It was bad enough that I had suffered the way I had for
so long, but now I didn't even have a name. I would go
to family functions and reunions, and oftentimes people
would want to know who you are because our family
was huge. But it was during this time I remembered
feeling like nothing more than a child of someone who
had taken someone's life. I know that in my family's
eyes this may not have seemed significant or relevant at

this crucial time in our lives but it was. Being accused, tried and convicted of a crime you didn't commit was hard. We were much too young to understand and hadn't committed any crime. It was crazy! Unfortunately, society has a way of unknowingly inflicting this verdict onto the children.

Many people do not realize how important a person's name is. It can speak life or death into that person's Spirit. So at these family functions, people would say, "Now whose baby is this," or "Who is your mama, baby?" I could remember on countless occasions where someone would answer and say, "You know that's Sue's youngest girl," or "That's Sue's middle child."

I didn't realize the significance of what that meant for many years later, but I often recall the person or people who understood would just say, "Ohhh!"

It was almost as if saying that we were Sue's child or children meant that we didn't have a name, purpose or any value. It was like saying I was a product of someone that had done something wrong and that was all they needed to know about me. Not how I was doing? How had I been? I am sure anything encouraging or supportive would have been welcomed but just an underlying "Ohhh." No speaking life into a dead situation but just simply "Ohhh."

How many times has society condemned someone because of something they heard? How about treating kids a certain way because of something their parents did? Or because of something they have done in their past? We were innocent children who had been wrongly convicted of a crime we didn't commit, and it was hurtful. I pray that if you have wrongfully convicted children or people in general for something their parents did as a result of what happened to them, you would reconsider and revaluate how you treat these children and others.

I inserted this chapter for this very reason. I heard a counselor tell me it was okay to grow up to be everything that had happened to me. I heard people carelessly take away what identity I did have failing to call me by my name. I am fearfully and wonderfully made, I am who God created me to be, and we know that God doesn't make mistakes. I am not what my mother did. I am not what happened to me, and I am loved.

God loves me so I pray that this chapter helps encourage someone, somebody, anybody or everybody. Stop condemning children and innocent people based on their physical condition or because of what happened to them. I was already a victim of severe physical, mental, verbal and sexual abuse. It is one thing to be physically abused but sexual abuse is serious because it impacts the person's spirit. It is something that is so devastating that it can take a lifetime for the wounds to heal and for the spirit to be restored.

> **Jeremiah 29:11**
>
> **For I know the plans I have for you,"**
>
> **declares the Lord, "plans to prosper you and**
>
> **not to harm you, plans to give you hope and**
>
> **a future.**

Recognize when a loved one needs help, and be there for them to ensure that they get the help they desperately need. This may help their wounds to be healed, repaired and restored. The Bible reminds us that there is power of life and death in the tongue. Therefore, we owe it to these children to at least call them by their names.

Simply because I prayed for their names and I call them by name joyfully and regardless of what anyone thinks about me, they have names that they answer to at all times. Never devalue what your name means, its significance or relevance. God's blessings begin at conception. See the two scriptures below:

> **Jeremiah 1:5**
>
> **Before I formed you in the womb I knew**
>
> **you, before you were born I set you apart;**
>
> **I appointed you as a prophet to the**

I was in my mid-twenties when this lady brought this to my attention. I am grateful that she posed this question to me because I had prayed heavily about what to name my children. I pray and seek God's guidance on every matter in my life. But I am thankful that God blessed me with the opportunity to have two beautiful daughters and to name them. So, regardless of what anyone said or does, they know who they are in Christ Jesus.

Since I lost my identity and had always had the lowest place value in the family, I think this is why some of the same sexual abuse continued from other relatives during this period of time. I had lost my identity, never knew who I was, and furthermore being "Sue's kid!" almost meant that people could do what they wanted especially to me, and it would not matter. I got the most whippings and stayed in trouble the most. I look back and realize I was screaming out for help I never got but desperately needed. They were performing what they considered "exorcisms" to deliver those demons out of me! Spiritually I had been violated so much who knows who or what spirit I had in me?
But, now I can stand boldly and say my name is Tiffany, I am Oneofakind, I am fearfully and wonderfully made, I am who I am, you are who you are, I am not you and you are not me, but I am exactly who God created me to be!

Psalm 139:14

14 I will praise thee; for I am fearfully and wonderfully made: marvelous are thy works; and that my soul knoweth right well.

4

The Aftermath

My mom served five years on what I think was a thirty year prison sentence in a maximum security prison. I know this is sad to say, but think of being in my shoes. I would always pray that they keep her in prison. Although my aunt pleaded and prayed that they would let her go free!

I know my aunt was probably sick and tired of us being there. I know they wanted us to write letters so the parole board would let her out. I know for certain they didn't want to use any of my letters to be used to help gain her freedom. I liked going to see her because I felt safe. She was in that place and couldn't hurt us anymore.

I don't remember all of what happened around her release. I thought our aunt wanted to adopt us. But I am certain her children were praying that my mom go free, and they could get their life back—what little life they did have after we had come and completely changed their lives!

My oldest cousin had to take on the role of being the man of the house and the one we looked up to while my aunt was not at home. On top of all of this, we had a handicapped sister who is older than all of us, but she was my mom's oldest as well. She had a lot of disabilities that we all had to assist with along with the younger kids in the home. Plus, we all had our unresolved issues. But society taught us to suck up and keep on moving. So, this is my story from my eyes. We all have a story.

My mom was on the brink of being released, and there were so many anxieties I experienced from adjusting to life with my aunt. But also I had the realization of what real love looked and felt like, and it was frightening to think about if my mom had changed. It was almost as if the sense of chaos I had once experienced was back. I don't remember all the details, but I know it was chaos.

We were removed from my aunt and weren't allowed to safely transition back with my mom. We were simply removed from this safe environment we had grown to love. We didn't know this woman known as our mom. All I had was all of the awful memories from before. I know that I wasn't excited about leaving my friends and the comfort zone with our aunt.

I confess I didn't like this feeling of uncertainty again It was scary. I kept thinking, Why are they letting her out? I learned that my mom had gotten married while in prison, and this made things worse. Maybe this time could have been used to help heal the wounds and the distant relationship between our mom and us.

But as expected she got out and took us from my aunt. If I recall correctly, because of this we lost all of our benefits. I still don't understand why parents always make decisions that are best for them but never best for the children. We had medical and dental benefits and were in the midst of the school year. I knew we were all unhappy about what happened because we had to move from where we lived in Tulsa, Oklahoma to live with my mom in Oklahoma City.

Although I don't have all of my memory about being in Tulsa, Oklahoma I knew that recently when I was reunited with some of those friends back in 2012, I surely missed them. I loved basketball and had become a great basketball player. Basketball and dance were my anti-drugs. They were comforting to me, and they kept me sane.

I knew that leaving those friends abruptly definitely had an impact on my life. It hurt. You know, never having friends that you could say you grew up with like other people hurt. But since hurting didn't help me, I sucked it up and kept it moving. As I explained, my heart grew smart: don't let anyone get close to it. If they did, there was a 99% chance they would leave or be removed, so I found ways to ensure no one grew close to me.

I cannot recall if we got to take our things or not, but from memory, I truly do not believe we got to take our things. I say this because all of the things we had didn't come to Oklahoma City with us. I was devastated to be back in a lifestyle filled with chaos. She was married to a minister and I think his kids were used to a man in their life and we were used to women being the mother and father in our lives.

My mom sat us down and basically explained that God had forgiven her for all the awful things she had done to all of us. She didn't feel that she owed us any explanation and she didn't want to talk about it. I admit I was disappointed because I know it would have restored my spirit, given me hope and helped me many years before now. But as usual, it was never about what was best for the kids. As long as it brought peace to their life, I remained angry and bitter, and she could care less.

We are in this small house with a mom and stepdad we don't know or respect, along with his kids. I look back at these times and shake my head at the fact that they thought this arrangement would work. It was so crazy in that house. My mom still had this prison mentality. She liked everything disciplined, cleaned and in order. Now, we were screwed up preacher's kids. Go figure. An image to live up to that I had no idea what the heck it meant by any means. One of my stepsisters and I got into a fight and eventually we started fighting together against other kids. My older sisters were sneaking out of the house at night doing all sorts of things. There were lots of pregnancies and lots of abortions. I often laugh at the fact that they ruined things for me. You ever see people get chance after chance after chance and then come the youngest one? Well, because they had messed up so bad, I felt no one ever gave me a chance.

I was miserable. Our clothes would come out messed up in the wash, which we didn't have much. It seems like there were speakers in our room because much of what we discussed in private was known in public or to my mom and her husband. How did they know these things that we were saying in the privacy of our room?

At some point, I don't know who left the house first. I do know that I felt bad for my little brother. My mom had taken his father's life and she looked at him differently. I heard that my mom hated me because my dad didn't claim me. I don't know how true that is, but it would explain the hatred I felt she had towards me for most of my life.

Our mail was being intercepted and coming up missing, because although our aunt wrote us, we seldom got those letters. How do our lives get so screwed up over and over? I thought. We had simply gone from bad to worse. We had to clean the house like we were in prison or in boot camp for the Army. We had church most nights of the week, and I am unsure if any of that helped our situation.

Well, my oldest sister and I had grown fed up and we plotted and vowed we had to get out of this place. We had some classmates who had a mom and two daughters. She had gotten us bus tickets to Texas under her daughter's names.

The morning of the planned escape, we had our stuff in bags like they were trash, so we opened the garage pretending it was trash. I cannot recall if we got on the bus with the bags or not. But I do believe we rode the bus and got off on the stop where our friends lived and hung out there until she would take us to the bus stop.

I remember us having to hide under her pile of dirty clothes as the police somehow came looking for us at her house. I am not sure if they alerted my mom that we never arrived at school or not. Maybe the bus driver told on us. I do know that we ended up at the bus station, on a bus and out of Oklahoma that day. My sister was of age so she was okay.

On the other hand, I was still about fourteen or fifteen years old, I believe. I had missed a month or two of school. Plus, we had heard that my mom advised the police my aunt had kidnapped us. Nonetheless, after months of hiding, I went back to finish the year out and was kicked out of the house. My brother and his wife took me in. But that was short lived because their marriage didn't last long. I know that I knew her, and she had been with him for some time as for dating. But somehow they went their separate ways, and I became a ward of the state of Texas living with her.

I felt I had to get a job to pull my weight although she gave me a place to stay. I was not her responsibility. I was a ward of the state, and she was simply my guardian. I got to do a lot of things that I liked to do, but working was a must.

If I didn't work, how would I have clothes and things I needed? Everyone else in my school had only to worry about making good grades and having fun. Well, I had to work, make good grades and do the sports I wanted to do. Everything regarding my future was up to me. I didn't expect much from anyone because I always felt my sisters had ruined any chances for me ever to be truly happy or successful. I always felt like pretty successful people started with a good support system, which I desperately needed but lacked.

My sister-in-law did the best she could with the fact that she was forced in a situation of taking care of her ex's little sister who no one wanted to help or had simply given up on me. I look back and cannot confirm if much of it still related to just me personally or the facts that my sisters had made a lot of mistakes along the way. A lot of people really tried to help them, and they continued to mess up. Maybe that is why everyone was so distant in providing the support I needed.

> "Often times, victims have to forgive and move on with no apology, as the accuser moves on with no accountability."
>
> ***Oneofakind Tiffany***

5

New State, New School, No Rules!

Over the past few years, I thought I had overcome some of the ugliest years of my life. But over the years of not feeling or being pretty and really never picked for anything, something happened shortly before coming to Texas. I had a few encounters with young boys at the school who told me I was pretty and they liked my freckles. Hmm, can you imagine that? Old ugly, nappy-headed Tiffany turned into a swan! I felt I had been given the short end of the stick. I was skinny, had nappy hair that wouldn't grow, and I had freckles. People with freckles are always on the butt end of connect-the-dot jokes, but I am truly that story of an ugly duckling that turned into a swan.

During this time, I had started to love myself and had actually started to look in the mirror. When life had left me, beat down, ugly and abused. You can carry this dead weight with you for a lifetime. I had been on the low end of the totem pole all my life, the black sheep of the bunch, and I had finally started to see the beauty in me.

So, now I am in a new state where I attended a new school, Lake Highlands High School in Richardson, TX. I loved the fact that I came out of nowhere and had nothing, but everyone embraced me. I could play baseball, and I ran track, so I just kind of fell in with the athletes. I think I knew a few people from the apartment complex where I lived, and that helped me get to know people.

My first job was at Wendy's, and I remember I walked to and from work on school nights, still made good grades and played sports. I had a few people that became what one would think were friends. But funny how you can have absolutely nothing and yet gain enemies from nowhere. So, I often got to listen and watch friends who had known each other for years and their interactions with one another. I became friends with a group of men and women, some who I am still in contact with today.

But there came a time when I had this one particular friend who kind of favored me in that we were pretty, thin and brown-skinned. She might have had freckles as well. I think at some point a guy she dated for some time took an interest in me or something to that effect. Unfortunately, it was not what she thought, because I was already dating someone else and never had an interest in her ex. That same year, I would meet a young man that would change my life. We became friends and before you knew it, he was my boyfriend. We were still in the early stages of dating when I was set up by this so-called friend.

I stayed the night at her house. I was at this friend's house in a room that I had slept in before. Sometime in the middle of the night, a young man was allowed into the house and in the room to rape me. No one ever knew much about the situation, because I was accustomed to being used and abused. My sister-in-law decided she wanted to move to Irving anyway, and that would give me a fresh start. I hate what happened to me, but it just seemed no matter what I tried to do and where I went, things just found a way to manifest themselves in my life.

I had made all these friends but because of my situation, I had to leave and go to school now in Irving, TX. I hated being in Irving and the school I had to go to. I was such a cold-hearted person but at the same time had a big heart. That is crazy to say cold-hearted and big heart, but that best described me during this time. I could be very hard on people because life had been hard on me. I felt if I could survive all I had gone through, so could they. But I could also be such a forgiving person. My mom came home from prison, and although I hated her for a long time, she had changed. She was not the way she had been with me in the many years before.

I still had this new boyfriend who had a very supportive single mother that was doing an awesome job at raising him. He was the ultimate gentleman to me. But it would be many years before I could fully grasp that he loved me because, sadly, I didn't know what love was. Love for me was always inconsistent, painful, and unstable. We were still boyfriend and girlfriend while I attended school in Irving. I played ball and ran track there because basketball, as I mentioned earlier in the book, was my first love. It was like my anti-drug. For me, things appeared to be going well although I strongly disliked this school in Irving. I hoped that I could switch schools my senior year so that I could go to school with the friends I had made at Lake Highlands.

My sister-in-law and her boyfriend were now expecting a child. In an apartment complex, if you have a child they took an occupancy spot on your lease. I know that we always lived in a one bedroom apartment. But I always had a blow up mattress or slept on the couch. Once her son came, I was advised I had to go, and was left homeless once again. This time, something really strange happened because while I was dating my boyfriend, his mom had paid attention to my drive and determination, and she soon offered to allow me to come live with them.

It's more common now than it was then but I am most grateful that she provided me a place to stay. She really tried to mentor, guide and direct me. but here I was a senior in high school, yet still so broken. She had no idea what I had gone through or the many things I had experienced. I had no major counseling and here I was in her home with no foundation for much other than determination and fight to make it and be something better than the hand life had given me. I know she took a risk on me, and it caused a lot of ruckus in her family by taking in this strange girl who happened to be her son's girlfriend. But also she had saved my life. Who knows where I would be had she not taken me in?

I attended a school I had grown to love with friends I knew and liked. Maybe their stability rubbed off and was comforting for me. Who knows? But their lives were not and had not been anything like mine had been.

6

A Walking Miracle

I had been molested, beat down, severely abused, depleted, raped all by the time I was about fifteen or sixteen years old. But what happened next for me did not even resonate in my spirit until recently. My pastor often says, "If it had not been for bad luck, I wouldn't have any luck at all!" Boy, this was my story. Until recently, heartache and pain were among the few constants in my life. They managed to follow me no matter where I went.

During this year, I had started seeing a doctor for birth control as well as for my well woman yearly exams. I was devastated when I got the news that I had been diagnosed with cervical cancer. Cervical cancer is very common for women who are molested early in life. The Doctor asked me if I had been sexually molested when I was younger. I didn't understand why I had to bring this up, but I explained that I had. This was another devastating blow for me at such a young age. I was devastated that I had cancer but so much more devastated when he said, "Once you have the surgery, you can not have kids, because you need to have a hysterectomy." Honestly, I didn't know or care about the chemo, radiation or hysterectomy. But I heard the part about never getting to have children!

Can you imagine going your whole life in a sense fighting to beat odds and avoid becoming a statistic? Yes, I had a bad attitude and a temper, and it caused me to fight a lot. Life made me angry and left me just cold-hearted. I taught myself that this was how you dealt with stuff. Now, cancer and no kids!

I recall growing up in the church and even went to a Caucasian church with my boyfriend and his mom. Heck, I don't even know to this day if it was a Baptist church or what the name of it was, I just know we went. But I began to pray to this man named Jesus that I had been hearing and learning about all these years. I begged and pleaded with him to please allow me the opportunity to have children. I was mad; I was upset that on top of everything, now this!

I had prepared for this surgery for weeks through biopsies and other tests. I rolled into Parkland that day, and I believe my boyfriend came with me to see me off. I don't think he understood what I was going through, because I am uncertain whether or not I had shared with

him everything the doctors had told me. I just
remember rolling into Parkland that morning, knowing
that my life was going to change forever. I wanted to
have kids so bad. I wanted to show the world what a
real good mommy looked like. I wanted to have an
opportunity to be called "Mom!" I rolled into Parkland
that morning but I was rolled back out. The doctor's
said we cannot explain what has happened, as we have
shown you everything up until this point.

He explained that the cancer was gone! I didn't
understand what all that meant in the first couple of
seconds. There are a lot of people had no idea that I
even went through this. As I stated, my only desire at
this point was the comfort in knowing I could be a
mother one day. I wanted to know what it felt like to
love a child and have them love you back. Many people
see children merely as dolls or puppets that you can
dress up, doll up and everyone "ooh and ahh," but it's
so much bigger than this. We are responsible for
training that child up and playing a vital role in which
they become as adults.

Recently, as I began speaking publicly, God took me
through this process of transformation in my life. He
brought this situation back to my remembrance. I am
just elated that God decided to allow me to walk away
completely healed of cervical cancer. Furthermore, in
my studying as a Health Care Administrator, I learned
that sexual molestation and/or rape in women is linked
to the HP Virus, which leads to cervical cancer. Once

again, just something else from my past that I felt had come back to haunt me. Every time something would be referenced back to my childhood, I would be haunted with nightmares for days and weeks afterwards. It would be of this broken little girl whose spirit was killed many years before.

It was just something additional I would have to worry about as a teenager. Every year it seems like if something happened and it was good, it would only last for a little while. Eventually, it would be tainted with some bad news. I didn't understand why or how my past had a way of just coming back up no matter how old I got or how far I had come.

As a result of the cervical cancer, I was told I would never have children. Yet, I walked away completely healed. I would have to have Pap smears more frequently than others, because they had no explanation for how I was completely healed. At first it was every six months, then every year, and eventually I was removed from the high risk list. It feels great to have received nothing but good test results every year since then.

The blessing even after many years of testing is that I have two beautiful daughters now. How amazing is God?

"Some people will only read of miracles, some people will experience miracles, while others, are simply a walking miracle!"

Oneofakind Tiffany

7

Becoming a Statistic

Sta·tis·tic

A fact or piece of data from a study of a large quantity of numerical data.
An event or person regarded as no more than a piece of data, considered as a number, not as an individual.

Now that I have survived all of these things within the pages of this book, I felt I was finally about to shake this thing and beat all odds. I was still living with my boyfriend and his mom through high school and had decided I would join the Army so that I would make something out of myself. I loved to play ball and I earned numerous accolades, awards, a lettermen jacket, and the title of MVP and most defensive my sophomore through senior years in high school between Irving and Lake Highlands.

I had already enlisted into the Army when I received a letter and call from Hampton University in Hampton, VA. It's the private HBCU, which stands for Historical Black College or University. But the letter advised I had earned a full scholarship for basketball and track at their University. I am not sure whether or not I would get to go visit or how the signing and all of that went, because kids like me really didn't have that support and help that we needed. I was a nobody, who came out of nowhere, and who was fighting just to be here. I felt that I had to be something or somebody to prove statistics wrong. I had been fighting my entire life and I was exhausted.

Yes, I had made it out of high school with no babies, so in my mind and in our communities, if you graduate it's like a sigh of relief for parents. They feel that their jobs are complete, and in all actuality a parent's job should be just beginning. Why are we so content with only making it out of high school with no kids? Look at statistics: most of us who make it out of high school find that an even greater number do not make it out of college without children. What about your career, your job and starting a family?

This would prove to be one of the most disappointing times in my life, but at the same token the most amazing. I was on break from college and was no longer seeing my ex-boyfriend because he had joined the Navy with his mom's support, and I was between the Army and Hampton University. Back then, they had the opportunity for you to do a split option to go to school. So I was able to start college in 1998 and serve in an infantry unit while at school in Virginia.

When I first joined the Army, I know people thought one of two things: she isn't going to make it because of her attitude, or that it will change her attitude for the good.

The first day at Boot Camp, I got in trouble. I remember it like it was yesterday because all it took was that one time before I realized I should never volunteer for anything else in the Army. Well, I had raised my hand to volunteer my writing skills to assist with a task before they actually said what they needed me for. Then they told me they needed me to hand write out about 250 soldiers' information. On top of all that, I had to make four copies.

I still laugh at the look on their faces when I told them, probably with a few choice words, that I was not about to do that! They had me ALL the way messed up! Ironically, that was not what any of them wanted to hear come out of my mouth. The main culprit was an Asian guy, and I remember there were about seven drill sergeants all yelling demands at me at the same time. But I could still hear DS Teope in my ear, saying "Pu private, Pu Private!" Now, I could not figure out what the heck pu meant, but I later found out he was trying to tell me to just do pushups until they told me to stop! Believe it or not, that was one of the few times I got in trouble in the nearly four or five months. I had become a model soldier at Ft. Jackson, NC, as a platoon leader and often led my platoon in cadence and other missions. I qualified on the gun range with both my left and right hand, and was one of the few women that had succeeded in being one of the top five soldiers out there. I am thankful for my time in the service. It made me a better person, completing eight years, becoming a recruiter assistant for two years before I ETS out of the service in 2005.

I was then off to college to enjoy this beautiful campus. I still have people I consider brothers from Hampton whom I have known for eighteen years. It was an awesome experience, and I am glad that I went, even against my family's wishes.

Virginia was twenty-four hours away. I had one cousin, Greg, who lost his life a year before I graduated from high school. But he was the only person who encouraged me to take the scholarship and head far away from my family. Now remember, for the most part, this family was not as supportive as I would have loved or liked but they were family, and we don't get to choose who our family is. But we are forced to love them whether near or far.

During a break I met a man who was living a double life, and I got pregnant. I received a letter from him making this confession, and I kept this letter for many years.

But when I went to the doctor's office, all the tests they ran came up negative. I was on a birth control called Depo-Provera that had clearly failed me. I even petitioned my sister's doctors for a second opinion, as I felt something was severely wrong since I was constantly nauseated and sick. But again, they all reassured me I simply had a stomach virus.

I'd met a friend at Hampton University who became closer than a brother. We called ourselves twins, because we had the same birthday. Since I was sick as a dog, he agreed to drive me back to Hampton with him. His brother went with us.

I still laugh about this adventure, because a couple of flat tires and a few days later we made it to Hampton. They still laugh that the reason for the two flat tires was because I had so much stuff packed in his car.

I went back to Hampton University, which would have been my junior year. I was throwing up so bad one day at a skating event we had. After being rushed to the emergency room by some of my girlfriends that I still know to this day, I learned I was pregnant. Naysa, Courtney, Michelle, and Nadiyah were friends I had grown close to while at Hampton. They were just as shocked as I was to learn I was pregnant. They didn't tell me how pregnant I was, so I assumed a "little" pregnant.

I made arrangements for an abortion, and you go in there with two money orders. You don't know why until you have to be rolled back out with one in your hand. The Doctor told me that it was illegal to have an abortion in Virginia after three months into your pregnancy. She even asked had I felt the baby kick yet.

I was sick as a dog. I had stopped eating because everything made me sick. I look at pictures I took at around six or seven months of being pregnant and my stomach was flat as a model. My eyes just looked tired.

I had recently moved off campus with a friend of one of my brothers from Houston, TX. They had a fight one night, and the police were called out. There was a standoff, and he wouldn't let her out of the apartment or anyone else in it. She came out many hours later, but confessed he had not kept her against her will, so the police had to let him go.

Soon after learning I was six months pregnant, my roommate stole everything I had while I was at church. I had just bought everything I needed for our new apartment. She even took all my personal belongings, which I had worked hard for during the years at Hampton.

I was left completely devastated! This period in my life when had I been at a place to hear God, I could have saved myself many more years of hurts, trial, and tribulations, but maybe I can help someone else. I was now very sick, very pregnant and very homeless. My friends I had made at Hampton helped get me to Atlanta and finally they got me back home to Texas.

It was hard because this was the first time I felt tired and mad with myself. I felt like I had let myself down and I was so disappointed in Tiffany! I had fought most of my life, getting by with what life had given me and things I learned along the way. Somehow, I still managed to become a statistic. How the heck did I let this happen?

Young black girl, no degree, homeless and pregnant. I was disgusted and disappointed in myself!

This was the first time I questioned my own existence . I asked God, "Why have I had so much suffering and pain at such a young age? I was so young and innocent. What had I done to deserve all these awful things that happened?"

God answered me: "People are still being crucified so others might be saved." It would take me years to understand this. I was just twenty-one years old.

8

Jia: The Gift

So, now I was home from Hampton, which my family had all agreed was a bad idea from the start. I cannot say if I wanted to do this personally to prove them wrong or because their opinion didn't matter, since they didn't play a vital role in my getting there. But they made it clear that they were completely disappointed in me and didn't want anything to do with me or the baby. They had felt that out of my mom's kids or girls I was going to be the one to make it.

Sadly, they were more or less six years late on that. I felt if I had a constant present, stable and loving support system, I would have known before that moment that they thought anything of me or had expectations for me. I was dealing with so many emotions. t I would tell my friends back at Hampton, "I am a tomboy and I am not having a baby!"

There was a song by Lauryn Hill called "Zion" that I would sing to my unborn child almost every day. It was the perfect love song to reject what I was being told by the doctors who told me it was better for me to get rid of her than to have her, and to my family who had turned their backs against me. But, I decided to suck it up and follow my heart.

I was pregnant and homeless. During this time I began looking for a church home like I had in Virginia. There was always a certain peace I felt while at church. I was twenty-one years old and pregnant when I became a member of NMZ Baptist Church in Dallas. I had not been in my apartment long and began taking the church bus to get there. I just knew I needed God's presence in my life despite my current condition.

I began to search for the guy I had been dating, Jia's dad, to advise him I was pregnant. I knew that a paternity test would be needed because, heck, who goes seven months and now you are out of nowhere pregnant? Of course, I was in Hampton and he was here in Dallas.

Nonetheless, after a few nights of sleeping on couches, he helped me get an apartment, and I got a job. I was so sick when I came from Hampton that the doctor advised it was in best interest of me and the baby to have an abortion.

I went to a class that was supposed to prep me for an abortion at six or seven months. This abortion would be medically based and was legal if they flew me to Las Vegas. As I sat in the class, I could not even finish the videos, they were so disturbing.

Who in their right mind kills a fully developed baby? They showed me some of the options of injecting something in my stomach that burned, slowly killed the fetus or induced your labor so you can deliver a dead baby. I was sick, and I mean I was so sick of everything that goes wrong while being pregnant, but I wasn't CRAZY! I nearly ran out of that place, facing the reality that I would have to give birth to her in less than four months.

I couldn't swallow my spit; I was depressed because I felt the baby could not be healthy because I hadn't eaten well for so long. I recall telling the Doctor, "Oh, no, I changed my mind." I worried about having a fuzzy navel daiquiri, that this would affect my baby! He reassured me if I agreed to move forward with having the baby she would be fine no matter how sick I felt. No matter how bad my feet swelled and my head hurt, the baby was getting what she needed.

I was preparing for a baby to come into this world, yet I had no furniture except a couch, television, and an air mattress. It was a struggle. Every time I got a check I would buy something I needed. Did you forget I was five and a half months pregnant when I was robbed of all my belongings? I admit I felt like my little girl's dad was heaven sent because my whole family had turned their backs on me during this time and he was there.

One time, I remember being at my aunt and uncle's house in Flower Mound while pregnant. I remember my family all feeling the need to tell me they were disappointed, and that is why they didn't care much for the baby or me. I remember just taking off walking sick and pregnant. I just realized that they simply hated me all my life, and there wasn't anything a baby could do to change that. I needed help to get things for the baby, but they guaranteed me they would not spend a dime on the baby or me.

I was so blessed though, in the short time, I worked at Blue Cross Blue Shield as a temp they really embraced me. I took about three buses each morning to get to work by six a.m. They even had an ottoman at work and allowed me to take small naps in the beautiful bathroom we had.

One day I came to work, and they had a big baby shower set up for me. They reminded me of how I had impacted them working while I was supposed to be on bed rest because of all the things that had gone wrong and made me sick while pregnant. They saw me riding the bus every day to work sick, pregnant, but doing what was needed to prepare for this baby. I was so blessed because the shower was so big, I got more than what I needed or wanted for the baby. It really helped me since my family had not been there for me. I got a baby bed, car seat, stroller, swing, clothes and diapers for nearly the first year.

They checked on me and often teased, "The morning you are not here at six a.m. we know it's because you had your baby." Well, they were surely right. On the Saturday before I had her, AT&T still had not turned on my home phone. I had started having back contractions, so I had to walk hunched over to the corner store and called my cousin. He gave me a ride to Parkland, and my other cousin that had been raised as a sister to me was there.

Since I refused to take medicine or epidural and my blood pressure kept going up and down, they kept me a little longer. I had dilated but I'm not sure how far. I was bleeding really bad and was in a lot of pain, but Presbyterian Hospital of Dallas later sent me home without my baby's delivery

A short time after they had released me on Sunday evening, I was back in the early hours of Monday morning. But this time, my water had broken, and my phone still wasn't on, so again I walked to the corner store. I arrived back at the hospital, and her dad and my cousins were there. The doctors predicted that I would not have her probably until later that evening. But after everyone had left and my cousin was sitting on the couch near me, I felt this pressure, unlike anything I had felt before. I sat up and screamed, "Oh shoot" for a lack of better words, and I started pushing. The doctors ran in telling me, "Don't push!"

It was as though my body was pushing without my permission. I told them to please take my hand. All the nurses and doctors refused. But my cousin did, and I think she regrets it to this day!

Beautiful Jia (pronounced Ji-ya) was born at 5:59 a.m. on Monday morning, July 17, 2000. She was only about 5.5 pounds and about twenty-one inches long.

It still amazes me that there are some things you just don't forget. I will never forget making that call to my coworkers advising them of the joke they made about me not being at work by six a.m. She came a minute before six a.m. I don't remember if many family members came to see her at the hospital outside of my cousins, but my coworkers did. She was beautiful, but she looked Asian to me. Before I moved to my private room, there was an Asian in the room. I told them they must have given me the wrong baby. I could not fathom that God will allow someone as ugly as I felt most of my life to have such a beautiful baby. She was my baby, and I was so protective of her.

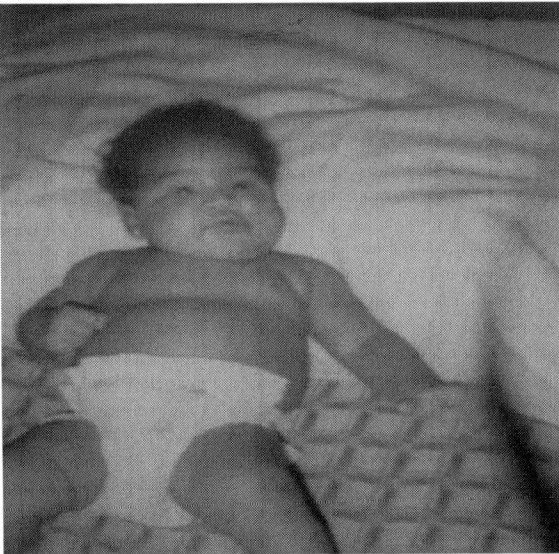

I remember her coming home and shortly after she did, I got a bed for me to sleep in. But she had a lot of stress on her and colic. She would not ever seem comfortable or happy and always cried. We later learned that someone held her while they were on their menstrual and according to the old wives' tale, this puts a strain on the baby. It would be months before we discovered this fact, but once we got the twine bracelets for her wrists and ankles it went away.

I had no support or help. One day I was taking a bath and Jia was crying. There was a knock at the door. When I opened it, it was my aunt that had raised us while my mom was in prison. She was heaven-sent and right on time.

As a result of the stress, I had suffered a setback which is what happens when you do too much after you have a baby, and it's almost like you are reliving your labor pains. I had seventeen stitches as a result of a natural birth. But I didn't want to relive that pain again.

I greatly appreciated my aunt, who drove from Oklahoma to see the baby and try to help me a little.

Jia changed my life for the better. Lord knows I had a fight a week before I gave birth to her because of my bad attitude, and fighting with my hands was in my nature. It was the way I was taught to deal with problems. It was just Jia and I, and I will always have a special place in my heart for her. She was innocently my life saver, and she didn't even know it. She changed my life, and I am blessed to have experienced giving her life after being healed from cancer.

There would be two opportunities when the enemy tried to steal her from me. At some point during her first year of life, she was being kept by a lady that lived in our apartments who was recommended and referred to me by the apartment office because she was a nurse. One day I saw Jia in the window, and I started having nightmares in which she would be falling out the window, and then I would wake up.

One day the babysitter had a death in the family, and she had left the door open and the gate to this room unlocked. Jia had wandered in there and, we assumed, she put her face to the screen looking out the window, and she fell about twenty two stairs onto the hard ground. She was not even one year old.

I received the call at work that day while were we were in a meeting. I told my friend that this dream was going to happen today, and that was them calling. She told me I was being paranoid. But often times I wished it were paranoia. The call was unlike any other from the ER at Presbyterian Hospital. She had been transported by ambulance because she suffered a fall out of a window.

Once again, I was devastated. My coworkers frantically drove me from Irving to Dallas with our hazard lights on. When we made it, I was hysterical. I could only see a beautiful face shattered or baby girl smashed. When I got there she was in a bloody shirt, but she only suffered a completely sliced tongue from biting down as she fell. The doctor said she had bitten straight through it during the fall. The doctors said we were lucky. She could have been permanently brain damaged, a vegetable.

There was an investigation launched by CPS and the police. A few months later I received a call to advise that federal charges were brought against the babysitter for posing as a nurse and negligence of a child.

The second attempt would come at the hands of a loved one. One day she needed a babysitter because her sitter had something come up. Can you imagine how paranoid I was? My past had me so scared to let her stay with anyone or allow her to leave my home. She was my baby, and if you wanted to see her or babysit, you had to come to my house.

This particular morning she had to be left with a male relative. I was a little hesitant, but it would only be for four hours as he had an appointment. I would come home at break and take them to my aunt. When I got to Jia, she was so resilient. She was so sweet she said, "Hey, mama!" She was now the apple of my eye. She had just turned two at the time of this incident.

Later that evening, I had gotten off work and went to pick her up. When I arrived, my aunt had her in the room, and my male relative was sitting at the table looking crazy. My aunt called me to advise my baby had way too many bruises on her. She pulled down her pants, and I lost it.

I ran to my trunk and pulled out my gun. I asked him what did he do to my baby and why? She had blood vessels ruptured in both of her eyes, which I later learned was from her crying and screaming so hard. I rushed her to Children's Hospital, where they kept her for three days.

They asked me what happened, and CPS was present to investigate. I didn't know, because I wasn't present when it happened. So the police ended up coming to my condo. They learned from two separate neighbor witnesses that late morning they heard her screaming! One neighbor said, "I heard her screams from over my loud music." He normally played loudly during this time. The other elderly neighbor said he also heard her screams at the same time. This confirmed I was at work at the time of the offense, according to the witnesses.

It was a very hard time for me, because I had done everything I could to protect her. I kept her way from people and always had people come to my home. Why do bad things always have a way of finding me? I pleaded with my family that this person needed help. Instead, there were questions brought up about my childhood. I thought, this is hurtful, but they have a lot of nerve. How the heck can you criticize when you never helped us when we were kids? They believed I had given him permission to spank her. Others felt I had done it because of my past, and the others didn't want to get involved.

I was devastated and heartbroken once again. I knew they didn't support me, never had and never will. But I was thinking, this is a two-year-old innocent kid. Are you serious?

CPS made their recommendation, and when no one wanted to acknowledge anything, I moved forward with pressing charges. Society, my family, and CPS never helped me as a child. I owed it to my child to let her know I did all I could, and I had her back.

After the incident, as a two year old she was wise and full of discernment as she made the decision not to see my family for a while.

How often are children abused in society and people do nothing? How often are innocent children abused by family members and people don't help or don't want to get involved? Eventually, that mentality is a disaster waiting to happen. In the end, God showed me something powerful as I lay crying out to him. "Why my child? He told me, "Tiffany, your problem is you think she is your child! She is not your child. She is mine. I loaned her to you, and when I am ready for her, I will take her back from you!" What a way to learn a lesson!

But that allowed me to put what it meant to be a good parent, mother or father in perspective. I am to love my children, and I am to put my trust in God to protect them. Jia means "beautiful" in Chinese. Jia and I went through some struggles, and I will always have a special love for her in my heart for those that love her and for those that do not. She is so smart and gifted even to this day. I have had random strangers tell me she will be great! But my God showed me that the devil knew this before she was even born as he laid down traps to end her life.

Jia, I pray that you will one day see that God has a purpose and plan for your life. I carried you for nine months and experienced every sickness one could encounter while pregnant. I lost everything while carrying you. I was homeless, talked about and criticized. I was very disappointed in myself, but GOD!

There were people in the family that had nothing to do with you for many years, and others not to this day. The love I have for you is BIG. God has blessed you intellectually and with many gifts and talents. I still stand in awe as I look at your résumé filled with many awards, achievements, and honors from Dallas to Washington, DC. To say that you are a leader is an understatement. You are one of the most talented, gifted, beautiful and smartest girls I know. God has blessed you with so many gifts. It's up to you to decide which ones to use and how. But make sure you remember that ALL GIFTS COME FROM GOD and HE GIVES AND HE TAKES AWAY! I pray that you will be all God has gifted you to be. I love you beyond measure, my first, my change, to the heavens and back always! I love you mostest!

I'll love you forever.
I'll like you for always.
As long as I'm living,
My baby you'll be!

9

Tiana: The Wise One

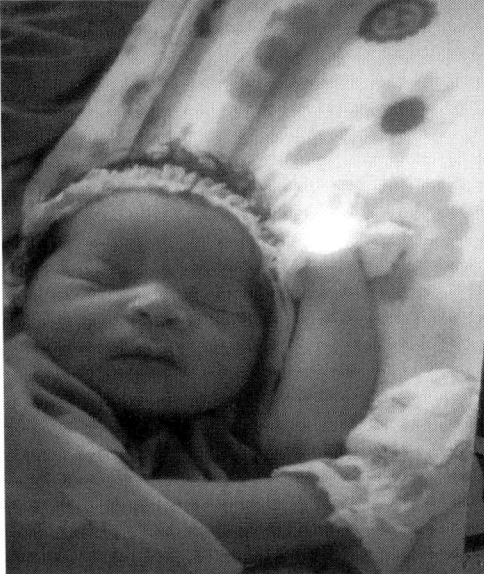

I have had some good days and bad days as we all have. In the time between Jia and Tiana, I was a dancer, became a model, actress and had some wonderful opportunities. But I realized I had turned into a beautiful person on the inside and outside, in spite of the many hurts I endured over my life.

I had the wonderful opportunity of working with countless celebrities, such a Li'l Wayne, 50 Cent, E-40, Master P, Steve Harvey, Floyd Mayweather, Vivica Fox, Christian Keys, Chris Brown, Paul Wall, and Clifton Powell., I had the opportunity to travel to many places, to grace many stages be it acting or modeling. I had a lot of wonderful opportunities modeling for different clothing lines from across the US, but for some odd reason I could not allow myself to fully engage in this life. We have read about it in the Bible, "to gain the whole world and lose your soul!"
I felt that I was having fun, being paid, traveling and taking advantage of all the opportunities that presented themselves, but my soul was not in it. I would eventually give it all up to work on my relationship with Christ.

It was during this time I reunited in communication with her dad. Somewhere as I was driving back from San Marcos, TX, God told me I would marry this man. It was crazy because I was like, "I am not marrying that man!" I mean, we hadn't spoken or seen one another in years. I felt that maybe because his mom was in ministry and my mom was a first lady, this would be a great mix because we would be on fire for Christ together. Little did I know the hell that would soon rob me of all my peace and joy that awaited me in this marriage.

It started out beautifully, praying, church, expecting a new baby and family. Now, imagine if it took me awhile to come to grips with marrying him, you know my family was like, heck, no! Funny, because I think I love my family, but my relationship with them over the years has been unstable and inconsistent. I felt that at one of my lowest points in life he was there where they were not, and maybe this was God's way of proving them wrong. Or was it?

He was a good person with a big heart, but he suffered from some serious addictions. I never had anyone near me that struggled with any addiction. He wanted to do right, but I realized if your heart and mind were not right, there's a big chance you would not change.

He got in trouble for driving me from work one day. I was really sick, and he was pulled over while driving. Needless to say, he went to jail. He struggled with much insecurity that in my opinion prevented him from standing boldly and confidently on his own behalf. Sadly, his family worshipped the ground he walked on and helped feed this addiction more than anyone else. I believe right is right and what is wrong is wrong, even for my own children or family. Of course this didn't help the situation. I was the only person bold enough to beg and plead with him that God had greatness in store for him, and had given him value and worth.

Everyone else was telling him he was okay, and that didn't help solve the problems. He was gone when I was about five months pregnant and did not return until a week before Princess Tiana was born.

I recall the night before she came, I had already moved Jia's tenth birthday party a week sooner than her actual date of the seventeenth because Tiana would not make her July 23rd due date. I was in labor a little after midnight, but I kept begging her to wait until Monday, so we could make it to sissy's party.

After calling the doctor, I was advised to drink thirty-two ounces of water, and if the contractions persisted, I needed to go to the hospital because the baby was on its way. I was drinking my third 16.9 ounces. of water when I realized it was time to give birth to my second child.

My pain tolerance allowed me to continue to mosey around the house and jump in the shower as my ex-husband and Jia ran around the house in a panic. I finally got into the car distraught that I would miss Jia's first birthday party. I am and will always be her #1 fan and to miss her party made me really hurt. But I got to the hospital, and I was waiting for them to park the car. The security lady said, "Ma'am, you are in labor, aren't you?" I finally confessed, and she got the wheelchair and took me to labor and delivery. It's funny that I agreed 100% to have a natural birth with Jia and really wanted to for Tiana, but I think I realized that wasn't a good idea, so I only wanted to see the epidural paperwork at that point. I was like okay, I am older and wiser now, so I'd rather enjoy a much more pleasant child birthing experience.

When I say this epidural gave me life, it did! For the first time I saw how some women have a lot of kids. With the exception of carrying them for nine months, this was pretty cool. My actual doctor was not on call that day, so I had the rough associate, and I was so mad! She was rough in the doctor's appointments that I had with her. I think she made Princess Tiana upset because I was comfortable and she was breathing fine, and Dr. Jones came and moved me completely in another direction.

There was more family this time, and everyone felt like whatever she did at that point caused the Princess to dilate no further. I was a little frightened because for several hours, every time she checked me there was no movement, and we couldn't hear her heartbeat, but they said she was fine. In the uproar of the morning, I had taken a prenatal vitamin but didn't eat, so I was pretty hungry. I was begging for ice, a cracker, anything all to relieve this hunger and nausea. I was being pumped full of medicine, which made me even more nauseated. I think on that last check she sent the family out, and because Tiana still hadn't moved, she decided they would need to do a Cesarean section.

As she moved the sonogram machine back into its place, I finally threw up! I call it the best throw up ever, because when she turned back around and I was throwing up, she saw the crown of Tiana's head. She went back out to tell the family I was about to give birth!

Princess Tiana arrived July 11, 2009 at 4:01 pm at 7lbs 9ozs and 21 inches long. I was feeling so good. The doctor had to tell me when to push because I was constantly telling my ex-husband to "take pictures, take pictures, make sure you get pictures!" Boy, did he get the memo. As people came to the hospital to greet Princess Tiana, everyone looked at these pictures in this camera.

The doctor was cleaning up the room when she dropped my placenta and my ex nearly passed out. She was startled by a code blue announcement was made "with the room number." In that one second, I realized how blessed I was that I had a beautiful, healthy baby girl. As the night began to wind down, I got the camera and looked at the pictures realizing his pictures were too good, and everyone who came got a glimpse. How embarrassing! It was from the side view, but he literally caught when her head crowned until her little feet popped out! But the fact that no one paid attention to me sitting there, but more to the glimpse of how good God, was made it a little better.

Jia had been praying for this little sister for about five years. She said God had answered her prayer. One of God's greatest blessings for me was the memory of giving birth to both my beautiful girls. When I gave birth to Tiana, I was reminded that all children are different. In an effort to warn me that Tiana may not be as gifted as Jia, I also heard parents saying they love their kids differently and some even said more than another child. I prayed long and hard about this, after I reflected on all I had gone through. But when I saw Tiana's little face there was no doubt I loved her just as much and simply as the real Princess Tiana.

Her papa called her the wise one! Unfortunately, I attended two funerals while I was pregnant with her and the old wives' tales advise you shouldn't attend a funeral while pregnant. My friend's stepdad and a coworker both passed on while I was pregnant, and Tiana came out with a very old spirit about herself.

Maybe it was when the woman in Macy's freaked out and got out of line, advising my five-month-old baby was looking at her weird! Or maybe on another occasion she simply cracked up laughing at another lady in the store. We could slowly see that she was wise beyond her years, while speaking clearly at around six months old and taking first steps at eight months. When she took her first step and put each of our hands together and looked at us like telling us to clap, she took a step. Then she proceeded to walk only after we had all clapped for her. This should have been a warning that this one was simply going to walk in her own calling and not in someone else's shadow.

Jia has accomplished many things starting at the age of four or five years old. Tiana has not missed a beat becoming who she is. She performed Easter and Christmas speeches as early as two that older kids didn't even memorize, moved to pre-kindergarten class at three, and gave people the confirmation that reincarnation does exist. She has always been wise beyond her years in things she notices, remembers, and how her mind works. I know that God has amazing things in store for you, Tiana. Mommy believes that you are the one that will take care of your mommy. You laid hands on me in prayer at the age of three years old. You are the most beautiful, smartest, sweetest, caring and wisest little girl that I know. You are truly a gift from above, and I am blessed to be "Tiana's mommy!" I hope that you will grow into your God-given gifts and purpose in this life. I love you mostest!

I'll love you forever.
I'll like you for always.
As long as I'm living
My baby you'll be!

10

My Road to Damascus Encounter

We were married three years and things were going
okay, but not as well as they could go in the marriage. I
was trying to remain a praying and sanctified wife, but I
was losing the battle. Maybe God needed me to get
with this man so he could get me to this place in him.

Or maybe I was being punished. It was during this time
I realized that we were not equally yoked. I thought
being equally yoked meant as long as we both believed
in God and were saved. But God had to show me that
there are different levels, and if you are not on the same
level you are not equally yoked. He had some
addictions that were bigger than any praying and
sanctified wife could handle. My life had begun to take
a downward spiral. He totaled out my car, brought extra
drama into my life, and robbed me of my peace and joy.

Although some of the issues were small in the
beginning, I learned that little things matter. If
something small is not fixed, over time it can become a
bigger issue. It was a lifestyle that took him away from
his family, his home and the church. This lifestyle
either leads to death or a prison sentence. He was smart
and kind but that meant nothing if God was not head of
his life.

I learned so much from my marriage and do not have
any hatred in my heart towards my ex. He is a reflection
of my past and played a key role in my "Road to
Damascus" moment! I am thankful to him for that. If I
had not married him, I would not be in this very special
place with Christ.

I can only try to take what I learned as a result and tell
someone else, "If it isn't right, don't do it!" Because of
my past, I have compassion toward people in general,
especially those society has counted out. I always felt
cast out, and that people felt I was inferior, no matter
how great I felt, no matter what I accomplished. I felt
life had kept me in this place, like I was stuck in this
place of mediocrity. But I always had a desire to help
others when I couldn't even help myself. Or maybe this
was the trick of the enemy that allowed me to repeat the
negative behavior on myself that had haunted me early
in life.

Once again, it was a very hurtful place to be in, but
during this time God had begun to deal with me. Things

had gotten so bad in the marriage. There was no peace, no joy, and I hated to see his face. I felt that if Satan reincarnated himself in the flesh, it would be him. He was very deceptive and manipulative. God would show me things in my dreams, but if I mentioned it, the look in his eyes was like, "How'd she know that?"

Again, the addictions and his demons were much too big for me. There are so many people that suffer from addictions, and families feel that a quick letter of intervention will help them. But in all actuality how many addicts actually stop that behavior after their loved ones pour out their hearts to them? Exactly. Not that many, and it's unfortunate because the addiction stems from something deeper. Common addictions are alcohol, drugs, cigarettes, and sex.

There is one addiction we often fail to hear about, and that is an addiction to earn quick money. Proverbs mentions this as something that the Lord hates and as an abomination that people overlook outside of homosexuality.

Proverbs 6: 16-19

16 There are six things the Lord hates,
seven that are detestable to him:
17 haughty eyes,
a lying tongue,
hands that shed innocent blood,
18 a heart that devises wicked schemes,

feet that are quick to rush into evil,
19 a false witness who pours out lies
and a person who stirs up conflict in the community.

Each time I read this in Proverbs, I think of being
married to him. He was doing really well for a time. He
went to school, and he worked. But I think when
something is in you and unresolved, it's only a matter
of time before it manifests itself. This marriage helped
me realize that I had a high pain tolerance level. I didn't
realize it at the time, but things that bother most
women didn't affect me much. I was very aware and in
control of my emotions and myself. It made me very
strong!

Well, one day I woke up and looked around at my life.
My peace, my joy and everything was gone. I had lost
everything: job, cars, and a sense of security all at the
same time. I had this so-called husband I married,
supported and loved. I was not the perfect wife because
I didn't know how to deal with an unequally yoked
spouse suffering with an addiction. I felt my prayers
weren't being heard, even though you read that
scripture "a sanctified wife sanctifies her husband" and
vice versa.

1 Corinthians 7:14
14 For the unbelieving husband has been sanctified
through his wife, and the unbelieving wife has been
sanctified through her believing husband. Otherwise

your children would be unclean, but as it is, they are holy. (NIV)

The fact is simple: if you are not equally yoked, RUN! I don't think that it is wise to marry someone, be involved with, or spend time with someone who's not on the same spiritual level. It is a recipe for disaster. His mom was a leader in the church, yet I swear he was Lucifer's twin. When times got tough he would keep praying but it just got worse. If God is not the third strand in your marriage, you are doomed to fail. This is a spiritual warfare, and you have to be mindful of who you allow in your home, heart and body.

I honestly felt that he married me to punish me. Maybe because while I was taking care of Jia on my own, he wanted me to send money to put on his books while he was in prison. Money contributed from the outside provides a prisoner access to better foods, snacks, toothpaste and other personal items. I never understood why someone makes poor choices, and over and over lands in jail. Why do they expect the families to spend their hard-earned money to help them? People are taking care of their kids and themselves but they get mad if their loved ones don't keep their prison financial accounts loaded with cash. If you are man enough to do the jail time, man up and do the time. Imagine how hard time would really be if they didn't have those extra things, and he truly had to realize what it meant to do wrong and the consequences you can suffer as a result. I cannot say that is the reason, but I felt that he had some deep hatred in his heart, an addiction, and needed help.

I am not saying that all people that are locked up are there because of something they did wrong. But for those of age who continue making poor choices, at what point does it end, or people get tired?

Nonetheless, there came a point where I looked up and realized this chump had come into my life and turned it upside down. I couldn't sleep, I had no peace, and I didn't know when the phone would ring at any time with more bad news. Sadly, some things some people will never realize, no matter how hard you try to help them.

I cannot say if he was taking drugs, but one day while he was sitting on the couch, I walked out the door, locked it, and drove off. As I circled the condo, I realized I had left my phone and came back into the house to get it. He came into the bathroom freaked out. "When did you come back in the house?" I realized something was wrong. The way my couch was positioned, you were facing the front door, so there was no way anyone could sit on the couch and not see the door open. This was one of many encounters with him that I care to speak about.

When you have people that do not love you enough to say you are wrong and you need to change, it's really sad. I felt I was in this battle alone to get him to see his value and worth. I looked up one day and had that weak girl moment were I was just screaming "OUT OF MY HOUSE! Get your things, your addiction, your mess, your lies, and all your baggage OUT MY HOUSE!"

That was the first night I slept in peace in years. Whew! I thought, "Here we go again, Tiffany! I married this man that I thought I would be my soulmate. I wanted to see him beat all odds and be all that God created him to be.

Have you ever felt like you wanted better for people than they wanted for themselves? I felt this way. I realized his issues were way too big for me! I was strong! Even considered myself "Army strong," but sometimes the devil is wrapped up in people so tough there is nothing you or a prayer can do!

No, I am not saying I was the perfect wife. I didn't know how to love someone after all that had been done to me. An evil I didn't know existed, but every time I turned around, something was going wrong in my life. I didn't want him to touch or be close to me. I could not trust him or anything that came out of his mouth.

Does anything look or sound familiar? My past has come back to haunt me again!

You are probably thinking, You married this man, so you got what you deserved! Well, reality struck me one day, and I had to suck it up as I always had and took whatever came to me as a result. I had to stand up like an eagle and weather this storm like a true soldier.

I was mad at myself and I called God out! Yes, I did! WHAT DO YOU WANT FROM ME? What is it? I was mad, and I lay on the floor that first day, hurt, distraught, in tears at a complete loss for words and no answers! I looked up and there was no one there for Tiffany. Vashawn Mitchell a gospel artist reminds us in his song "Nobody Greater," that there is no one who stands with us like God in his grace, love, and mercy.

I was hurt to look around and see people that I had helped or supported take glory in my failure. I heard the words, I heard the laughter, and I saw the stares as I had to take a ride that would change the rest of my life. This was one of the lowest moments I had ever experienced. I was alone and hurt, but somehow I have always found peace in Jesus. And for the first time, I began to seek God only as it related to my current situation. I asked him to show me things I needed to see and people that were not for me. The more he began to show me, the closer I got to him. Eventually, I put down the microscope and used the mirror as a reflection of myself. I knew that my ex-husband was the reason for the demise of the marriage! He was the common denominator, but that didn't help me or my situation. So it was much easier to take the mirror and say, Lord, teach me, show me what I need to change. Show me people that are no good for me.

I had lost my job, and I didn't get unemployment. I had two children to support, and I had no income. I was doing all sorts of jobs in the meantime while I waited on a job to come through. I was also a full time student and single mother.

Be careful what you ask God for, if you are not prepared for the answer! His truth will lay you on your back! I felt like Ebenezer Scrooge in the Christmas Carol. He began to take me on adventures in my dreams where he would show me people and take me back to situations from the past. He showed me that some people were not really for me at all. He showed me that I had sacrificed, given up my life, taken risks for other people that wouldn't even get their feet wet for me!

I needed this awakening, or I would still have these people positioned in my heart. I had never let people get close to my heart. He had to show me that some people you have to pray for and let them go. Some people cannot be attached to your life and for others, the season had ended.

Family was scarce, so I called friends who took the opportunity to try to make my children feel they were lower because of my current situation. Everywhere I turned, it was one bad blow after another. I had begun to cry again, and Lord knows I was not a fan of crying. I was alone and hurting. I had two beautiful girls that I was responsible for, and they didn't know how I felt. I was seeking God's face, his direction and guidance every step of the way. Here are some songs that I would lay, pray and sing for days, for example "Greater is Coming" by Jekalyn Carr or "Sooner or Later", by Leandra Johnson. Tasha Cobbs, "Break every Chain." There were a lot of songs, stories, prayers and praise that took me from lying prostrate on the floor to sitting on my knees. Each day I felt I was getting a little stronger, a little wiser and a little better. I was going through a hard time and not many people knew.

I remember when people in the church were filled with the Spirit they felt one another's pain. They could look in your eyes and see your pain. I heard pastors say, "Someone over here is experiencing something in their body. It's on their left side. If it's you, come on down and let me pray with you!"

But you don't find the spirit in people these days. Sometimes I think people confuse their spiritual gifts with being spirit filled. I truly feel that there is absolutely no way you can have a true encounter with the spirit and remain the same.

Christmas came and went, and my oldest knew that things were not the same. She said, "Mama, we are good and have all we need!" I had people from the village look out for the girls for Christmas gifts. I kept kids after school for extra money, but was doing a lot of ripping and running.

I remember the time the bank called to say that I was in the negative. I had been with this bank since I was in the tenth grade. Mind you, I had lost my job, and I had gotten one check approved by unemployment before the company ironically came up with new evidence they didn't have three months before, and deposited $3,600 in my account!

I told my case worker, "It seems that if they owed me this money, why would it would it take three additional months to come up with new accounting?" I had a lot of stuff on auto pay and nothing coming in, and no more unemployment, so my account balance was negative.

I was terrified to answer another call from them. I was thinking, Lord, what am I going to do?

The next day they called me back. Still scared, I ignored the call. So it was about a week later when I finally checked the voicemail and they said, "Your account has been cleared since the deposit covered the negative balance!" I waited another three to five days for them to realize they had deposited $3,600 into the wrong bank account.

The call never came, so I finally called them and apologized to the representative and explained, "I don't have any money and I'm not expecting any. I believe the money you called about is not mine!" We researched back more than a year, and I had not received a deposit from that company before, but the deposit was legitimate. Can we say God still works miracles? This happened again about three months later.

Then just a month before that, I had been informed I had a case of identity fraud as a result of a license being stolen back in 2005. I would need to pay thousands before they would release the hold on my license.

I felt that no matter where I turned, things just went from bad to worse. I felt like I was on a darn roller coaster ride from hell. I was being punished and I had to take it like a big girl. I could no longer run from it. I had to face it. I took full responsibility for it and began to ask God to show me what I needed to see.

I don't care how much time and love you have for people, it doesn't mean that they are intended to be with you for a lifetime. I don't care how bad it hurts, but learn the difference between a season and a lifetime. **I said, "When people tell you something, you can listen and allow them to show themselves, but when GOD shows you something, you better believe him!"**

I had to walk away from some situations that ended up blowing up in my face because I didn't listen to God. I asked him for this, and when he answered I wasn't even ready to handle all he had to show me. I tell you, the truth hurts. Some people will not like you and not even understand you.

I figure if I was supposed to be like anyone else, then the first nine years of my life would have been different. I cannot change that, and I don't try to change it anymore. I am who God created me to be, and that's it. I felt I was in the valley for a year or two. You think of the Bible stories of the woman with the issue of blood or the crippled man at the pool. I had been dealing with some of these hurts for over thirty years. I had been running from what I didn't even understand.

11

My Road to Damascus Encounter Continued

God took me from the floor, to my knees, and back on my feet again. I began to realize that he really needed me to marry this man, to get me to this place in him. I had been running all my life. I had never stopped to grieve, to hurt, and to get close to anyone. I just kept it moving. Life had hurt me so bad. I felt like if I ever slowed down long enough I would be paralyzed with grief. I was still in this valley but there was a glimmer of hope as I got an opportunity to work in healthcare and put my degree to good use. I spoke to the recruiter who reminded me in order to get into healthcare, you may take four steps back to get two steps ahead. I felt that was typical in a career change. I was excited I got in and things were going better.

I finally finished school and obtained my Bachelors of Science from The University of Phoenix in Healthcare Administration and Management July 2013. I had to drop out of college back in 2000, and here I am thirteen years later finally finishing what I started. God was working on me, and I wanted to ensure he got the proper credit. I was glad to see that many of my family members showed up to support me for the first time. I finally made the corner as I had so many times for others, in celebration of the accomplishment. Many of them didn't even stay to hug or say, "I am proud of you."

A few months into the new job, the reality struck that my marriage was finally over, and he decided he no longer wanted to help in any capacity. There were threats and all sorts of additional stress brought into my life such that I just wanted that chapter to be over. I had to make a choice: the car note or daycare. I lost my car, but a family member was able to lend a car that had been sitting and was not running. The timing was perfect, as income tax season had rolled around. But this season was so crucial. I had just gotten a job and money was scare. I would need to use this money for savings. Sadly, the enemy took a situation and had it so far twisted that I'd rather have nothing to do with anyone associated with the matter. I had to spend the majority of the money I desperately needed that year to fix the car and pay her for the worthless piece of junk.

But at this point I realized, with my mom's help, that this was a spiritual matter, not her against with me or vice versa. This scripture will prove to be one of my favorite.

[12] For our struggle is not against flesh and blood, but against the rulers, against the authorities, against the powers of this dark world and against the spiritual forces of evil in the heavenly realms. Ephesians 6:12

God is still working on me. This is a process that had taken years to get me to this place. So, I guess he needed that much time to transform my life. This one scripture reminds you of how the enemy can use you when you do not have an authentic relationship with Christ. If you are dealing with people who are not equally yoked, the enemy will try to use them. Even in knowing this fact, God still needed to deal with me in these matters with myself and this relative. I was left hurt and devastated even though God had shown me some things that were coming to pass. I couldn't believe that things he showed were a warning. You learn that warning comes before destruction. He showed me and gave me answers to what I was asking. It was so hurtful I didn't believe it myself. So when I didn't take heed, it blew up in my face with each person for whom he showed me things I had asked.

I know that I needed to get to this place in Christ. Sometimes people and life will make you feel like a mistake you have made cannot be turned around. I feel that we all have our road to Damascus moments, but the outcome depends on who and what you turn to in that moment. Do you look for others to rescue you, or do you find ways to avoid dealing with the consequences? Yes, life had dealt me a bad hand early in life, but I learned to suck it up and keep it moving. I had so many unresolved matters that it would take something major for God to open my eyes and get my attention. He would and he did.

Often if someone is going through a struggle, we feel that we are in a place to judge why they are going through that situation. But in the twinkling of an eye, their situation could be yours. So it's best to pray before you say! In other words, pray for people before you start speaking about their life and matters you are not in a place to judge. Better yet, there is an old song that reminds us to sweep around our own porch before someone else's. The Bible tells us in Matthew 7:3-5:

"Why do you look at the speck of sawdust in your brother's eye and pay no attention to the plank in your own eye? [4] How can you say to your brother, 'Let me take the speck out of your eye,' when all the time there is a plank in your own eye? [5] You hypocrite, first take the plank out of your own eye, and then you will see clearly to remove the speck from your brother's eye." (NIV)

God advised me there were some things he needed to do so people would need to see me suffer. I was going to have to hurt in order to get this healing. I felt alone and so mad at myself for putting my kids in this situation. But God quickly reminded that the blessing of a child is at conception. Regardless of the facts surrounding childbirth, whether it is within a marriage or out of wedlock, they are a blessing. We fail to understand that the child is not the sin; fornication is the sin.

I was embarrassed riding around in a raggedy car. I was disappointed that feeding my kids was a struggle. It made me sad that I had to endure this valley experience and process to get to this place that God needed me to be. But I had to suck it up for real this time. Not suck it up and keep it moving as I had grown pretty successful at doing so. But suck it up, learn and grow from it. In this life, I feel, you either win or you learn and only when you fail to learn do you actually lose. God's word promises that he will never leave nor forsake us.

I would be lying if I said it didn't hurt like hell, because it did. I was happy the year I was off work. I got to spend more time and at the school for the girls. But I admit that sense of security I once had was lost. I had grown so dependent on Tiffany sucking it up, figuring it out, that I had forgotten that the only person who can do it better than any of us is God. He is the author of multi-tasking and getting the job done. The Bible says in Psalm 121:2-4, "My help cometh from the LORD, which made heaven and earth. He will not suffer thy foot to be moved: he that keepeth thee will not slumber. Behold, he that keepeth Israel shall neither slumber nor sleep.

If you are reading this book and whether you caused the disaster demise or it happened to you, God is love and a forgiving God. As long as you have breath in your body, you are never too old to live and dream again. It didn't kill you, and if you would seek his face, you will find him. Look around at the signs of the times; it is seriously time out for playing with God.

If you are professing Jesus Christ and his word, yet your life is not being transformed, I pray for you. There isn't a way that you can have an authentic encounter with Jesus Christ, the Holy Spirit or God and remain the same. I am not the only person that had a Road to Damascus encounter. Acts 9:1-19 tells the story of how Saul was on the Road to Damascus when his life was transformed.

Saul's Conversion

9 Meanwhile, Saul was still breathing out murderous threats against the Lord's disciples. He went to the high priest [2] and asked him for letters to the synagogues in Damascus, so that if he found any there who belonged to the Way, whether men or women, he might take them as prisoners to Jerusalem. [3] As he neared Damascus on his journey, suddenly a light from heaven flashed around him. [4] He fell to the ground and heard a voice say to him, "Saul, Saul, why do you persecute me?"

[5] "Who are you, Lord?" Saul asked.

"I am Jesus, whom you are persecuting," he replied. [6] "Now get up and go into the city, and you will be told what you must do."

[7] The men traveling with Saul stood there speechless; they heard the sound but did not see anyone. [8] Saul got up from the ground, but when he opened his eyes he could see nothing. So they led him by the hand into Damascus. [9] For three days he was blind, and did not eat or drink anything.

[10] In Damascus there was a disciple named Ananias. The Lord called to him in a vision, "Ananias!"

"Yes, Lord," he answered.

[11] The Lord told him, "Go to the house of Judas on Straight Street and ask for a man from Tarsus named Saul, for he is praying. [12] In a vision he has seen a man named Ananias come and place his hands on him to restore his sight."

[13] "Lord," Ananias answered, "I have heard many reports about this man and all the harm he has done to your holy people in Jerusalem. [14] And he has come here with authority from the

chief priests to arrest all who call on your name."

[15] But the Lord said to Ananias, "Go! This man is my chosen instrument to proclaim my name to the Gentiles and their kings and to the people of Israel. [16] I will show him how much he must suffer for my name."

[17] Then Ananias went to the house and entered it. Placing his hands on Saul, he said, "Brother Saul, the Lord—Jesus, who appeared to you on the road as you were coming here—has sent me so that you may see again and be filled with the Holy Spirit." [18] Immediately, something like scales fell from Saul's eyes, and he could see again. He got up and was baptized, [19] and after taking some food, he regained his strength." (NIV)

My plea to you is simple. Of course, no one wants to hurt for their healing to take place. Heck, I imagine if all of us could go through life without going through hurts, pains, trials or tribulations, we would. Sometimes the hurt, the pain is necessary in order for the transformation to take place. In John 16:33, "I have told you these things, so that in me you may have peace. In this world you will have trouble. But take heart! I have overcome the world." (NIV) During this season, I can only give God 100% responsibility for helping me back on my feet. Sometimes he has to get you to yourself. He has to eliminate all distractions so you can hear him and seek his face. If and when you do so, only then will you truly find him. Joy and peace are where he is but love is who he is.

Matthew 6:33

"But seek ye first the kingdom of God, and his righteousness; and all these things shall be added unto you." (NIV)

12

Favorite Scriptures that Helped Me along the Way

I would be remiss if I didn't tell share this list of favorite scriptures that I made as a result of going through this transformation. I hope that as you read and study these scriptures that just maybe they will touch you or have an impact on your life in such a way that you will be inspired to change.

Jeremiah 29:11 -13
For I know the plans I have for you," declares the Lord, "plans to prosper you and not to harm you, plans to give you hope and a future. 12 Then you will call on me and come and pray to me, and I will listen to you. 13 You will seek me and find me when you seek me with all your heart.

Isaiah 54:17

17 No weapon formed against you shall prosper, and every tongue which rises against you in judgment you shall condemn. This is the heritage of the servants of the Lord, and their righteousness is from me, says the Lord.

Jeremiah 1:5
Before I formed you in the womb I knew you, before you were born I set you apart; I appointed you as a prophet to the nations.

Ephesians 6:12
For our struggle is not against flesh and blood but against the rulers, the authorities and the powers of this dark world and against the spiritual forces of evil in the heavenly realms.

Romans 8:28
And we know that in all things God works for the good of those who love him, who have been called according to his purpose.

2 Chronicles 7:14
14 If my people, which are called by my name, shall humble themselves, and pray, and seek my face, and turn from their wicked ways; then will I hear from heaven, and will forgive their sin, and will heal their land.

Psalm 139:14

14 I will praise thee; for I am fearfully and wonderfully made: marvelous are thy works; and that my soul knoweth right well. (KJV)

John 1:1
In the beginning was the word and the word was God and the word was with God.

John 3:17
For God sent his son not to condemn the world but so that through him the world would be saved.

Isaiah 40:31
Those that wait on the Lord shall renew their strength; they shall run and not get weary, they shall walk and not faint.

Proverbs 3:5-6
Trust in the Lord with all your heart and lean not on your own understanding; in all your ways submit to him, and he will make your paths straight.

Ephesians 3:1-13
There is a time for everything, and a season for every activity under the heavens:
2 a time to be born and a time to die,
 a time to plant and a time to uproot,
3 a time to kill and a time to heal,
 A time to tear down and a time to build,
4 a time to weep and a time to laugh,
 a time to mourn and a time to dance,

5 a time to scatter stones and a time to gather them,
a time to embrace and a time to refrain from
embracing,
6 a time to search and a time to give up,
a time to keep and a time to throw away,
7 a time to tear and a time to mend,
a time to be silent and a time to speak,
8 a time to love and a time to hate,
a time for war and a time for peace.

2 Corinthians 4:8-12
8 We are hard pressed on every side, but not crushed;
perplexed, but not in despair; 9 persecuted, but not
abandoned; struck down, but not destroyed. 10 We
always carry around in our body the death of Jesus, so
that the life of Jesus may also be revealed in our body.
11 For we who are alive are always being given over to
death for Jesus' sake, so that his life may also be
revealed in our mortal body. 12 So then, death is at
work in us, but life is at work in you.

Luke 22:42
"Father, if you are willing, take this cup from me; yet
not my will, but yours be done." 43 An angel from
heaven appeared to him and strengthened him. 44 And
being in anguish, he prayed more earnestly, and his
sweat was like drops of blood falling to the ground.

Romans 12:1-2
Therefore, I urge you, brothers and sisters, in view of
God's mercy, to offer your bodies as a living sacrifice,

holy and pleasing to God—this is your true and proper worship. 2 Do not conform to the pattern of this world, but be transformed by the renewing of your mind. Then you will be able to test and approve what God's will is—his good, pleasing and perfect will.

1 Corinthians 2:9
But as it is written: "Eye hath not seen, nor ear heard, neither have entered into the heart of man the things which God hath prepared for them that love Him."

Matthew 6:33
But seek ye first the kingdom of God, and his righteousness; and all these things shall be added unto you.

Philippians 4:6
Do not be anxious about anything, but in every situation, by prayer and petition, with thanksgiving, present your requests to God.

Matthew 5:3-12
The Beatitudes
3 "Blessed are the poor in spirit,
 for theirs is the kingdom of heaven.
4 Blessed are those who mourn,
 for they will be comforted.
5 Blessed are the meek,
 for they will inherit the earth.
6 Blessed are those who hunger and thirst for righteousness,

for they will be filled.
7 Blessed are the merciful,
 for they will be shown mercy.
8 Blessed are the pure in heart,
 for they will see God.
9 Blessed are the peacemakers,
 for they will be called children of God.
10 Blessed are those who are persecuted because of
righteousness,
 for theirs is the kingdom of heaven.
 11 "Blessed are you when people insult you, persecute
you and falsely say all kinds of evil against you because
of me. 12 Rejoice and be glad, because great is your
reward in heaven, for in the same way they persecuted
the prophets who were before you.

1 Peter 5:10
And after you have suffered a little while, the God of all
grace, who has called you to his eternal glory in Christ,
will himself restore, confirm, strengthen, and establish
you.

Romans 8:30-31
And those he predestined, he also called; those he
called, he also justified; those he justified, he also
glorified. What, then, shall we say in response to these
things? If God is for us, who can be against us.

1 Peter 2:9
But you are a chosen people, a royal priesthood, a holy
nation, God's special possession, that you may declare

the praises of him who called you out of darkness into his wonderful light.

1 Peter 3:9

Do not repay evil with evil or insult with insult. On the contrary, repay evil with blessing, because to this you were called so that you may inherit a blessing.

Ephesians 4:4

There is one body and one Spirit, just as you were called to one hope when you were called; 5 one Lord, one faith, one baptism; 6 one God and Father of all, who is over all and through all and in all.

James 1:2-6

Consider it pure joy, my brothers and sisters, whenever you face trials of many kinds, 3 because you know that the testing of your faith produces perseverance. 4 Let perseverance finish its work so that you may be mature and complete, not lacking anything. 5 If any of you lacks wisdom, you should ask God, who gives generously to all without finding fault, and it will be given to you. 6 But when you ask, you must believe and not doubt, because the one who doubts is like a wave of the sea, blown and tossed by the wind. 7 That person should not expect to receive anything from the Lord. 8 Such a person is double-minded and unstable in all they do.

Hosea 4:6

My people are destroyed for lack of knowledge

John 8:32

The truth will set you free.

John 8:32

In this world you will have trouble, but take heart! I have overcome the world.

Proverbs 4:23

Above all else, guard your heart, for it is the well spring of life.

John 14:27

Peace, I leave with you, my peace I give you. I do not give you as the world gives. Do not let your hearts be troubled and do not be afraid.

Romans 12:2

Do not conform to the pattern of this world, but be transformed by the renewing of your mind. Then you will be able to test and approve what God's will is—his good, pleasing and perfect will.

1 Corinthians 10

No temptation has overtaken you except what is common to mankind. And God is faithful; he will not let you be tempted beyond what you can bear. But when you are tempted, he will also provide a way out so that you can endure it.

Proverbs 22:6
Train up a child in the way that they should go, so when they are older they will not depart from it.

Proverbs 1:7
The fear of the Lord is the beginning of knowledge, but fools despise wisdom and instruction.

Proverbs 4:7
The beginning of wisdom is this: Get wisdom. Though it cost all you have, get understanding.

John 16:33
"I have told you these things, so that in me you may have peace. In this world you will have trouble. But take heart! I have overcome the world."

13

Epiphany: God really Loves Me

After I had gotten to a point where I could stand again, God was still working on me. The process is necessary to get you to a place where he can use you. I was tired of doing things my way, yet getting the same results. I had hit rock bottom and had the nerve to call God out!

But it was in those moments of lying prostrate in tears, prayer, praise and worship that I got to know him best. I not only sought his face, but I established a relationship with him. This was the best thing I could have ever done. I had lived the part-time Christian life. You know, where you live for him part-time but expect full benefits. I posed that question years ago, and I pose it now. Why do we feel we are owed all of God's blessings but don't want to commit full time?

It makes you think of your employer and your benefits. In order to receive benefits, you have to meet the criteria of what it means to be a full-time employee. So in other words, no employer will give you full benefits working part-time. But I have lived that life and I know what it looks, feels, smells and acts like, and in the end, it's not worth it. I encourage each of you not to wait to make a genuine change until it takes everything from you, you're lying in the hospital bed, or your life is in the hands of the court.

It was in those years that God began to show me that he loved me so much. We all know that God is love, and he loves us because he died on the cross for our sins while we were yet sinners. I know love in that aspect, but I am talking about a love that is understood even when you are in the valley. It's easy to feel love or to love when the going is good, but how about when it's bad? It was an epiphany for me because I had never absorbed what that meant. He began to change my perspective. See, all my life, I had given the devil the victory by being angry and mad at the world. Then, even when I began to share my story, it was about my awful childhood. God began to show me you can either look at the glass half full or half empty. How long have you looked at the glass half empty? So long that you cannot see the real meaning or blessing? God's point exactly!

He told me, "Tiffany, even back then, my child, when it looked and felt ugly, I was there, and I loved you." All these years I looked at the glass half empty instead of being half full. God showed me that he loved us so that he gave up his only son to save our souls. Something happened when I began to realize how much he really loves each and every one of us. Think about when you are engaged to be married, you want the world or at least close family and friends to know and support you. Well, that is how God's love is supposed to be for us. We should be so wrapped up by his love that we want to share that same compassion and love towards others. We hear people say all the time, love people and trust in God.

"It is better to trust in the Lord, than to put confidence in man." (Psalm 118:8)

Then we are also reminded, "And above all things have fervent love for one another, for love will cover a multitude of sins" (1 Peter 4:8).

There are countless scriptures that serve to remind us to love our neighbors.
"You shall love your neighbor" (Leviticus 19:8, Matthew 5:43, 19:19, 22:39, Mark 12:31, 33, Luke 10:27)

When I realized that God was there all those years, and he kept me because I am alive today, I fell more in love with him. In this life, we will face trials of many kinds. I don't think the hurts were intended to hinder us but to help us. Think about it, those days are coming, but what we can learn from them is vital.

The fact that when Daniel was in the lion's den he didn't get eaten; Shadrach, Meshach and Abednego in the fire but didn't get burned; Jonah in the belly of the whale but didn't get consumed; and Job lost all he had and loved but didn't lose his mind. God's timing is the right timing and sometimes we don't like the bad and the ugly, but sometimes it isn't about you. Sometimes, he is using you to help or bless someone else.

God is not only patient, but he has basically given us a prescription to model in learning what love is. Well, if you haven't gotten the picture by now, I love for you to read and spend time in God's word. So therefore, mostly every scripture becomes my favorite, especially when I can apply it to my life and use it to make me a better person. Honestly, this has to be one of my favorite scriptures. 1 Corinthians for me takes his love to another level. We all know love because God is love and he died on the cross for our sins. Yes, indeed but to get an imprint of how we should apply the love he has shown towards us is amazing.

1 Corinthians 13:4-13
4 Love is patient, love is kind. It does not envy, it does not boast, it is not proud. 5 It does not dishonor others, it is not self-seeking, it is not easily angered, and it keeps no record of wrongs. 6 Love does not delight in evil but rejoices with the truth. 7 It always protects, always trusts, always hopes, and always perseveres.

8 Love never fails. But where there are prophecies, they will cease; where there are tongues, they will be stilled; where there is knowledge, it will pass away. 9 For we know in part and we prophesy in part, 10 but when completeness comes, what is in part disappears. 11 When I was a child, I talked like a child; I thought like a child, I reasoned like a child. When I became a man, I put the ways of childhood behind me. 12 For now we see only a reflection as in a mirror; then we shall see face to face. Now I know in part; then I shall know fully, even as I am fully known. 13 And now these three remain: faith, hope and love. But the greatest of these is love.

This scripture confirms why it is better to trust God, because he is love and his word says in John 14:15 & 23, "if you love me then you will keep my commands." So, he's telling us how we should take the love he has toward us and use it in our dealings with other people. It's simple.

1 John 4:20 says,
Whoever claims to love God yet hates a brother or sister is a liar. For whoever does not love their brother and sister, whom they have seen, cannot love God, whom they have not seen.

I cannot say what it does for you, but something happened for me the day I realized he really loved me. It's as if I went from confident to Godfident. I mean heck, honey, God loves me and because he loves me, I cannot even be mad at you.

I look back over my life and look at all the hurt and pain that I had to overcome. I was hurt physically, spiritually and verbally, but I am still here. I could have been out of my right mind, but I am sane. I love and I forgave even when it was not given in return. At some point, to get the healing you need, you are going to have to come face to face with those things, those people, and those issues and move on.

14

Hurt to Heal

Finally, these were the most powerful steps in the process. I did a presentation a year ago as a Healthcare Administrator about moving toward early prevention and detection. In the presentation, I provided a handout, and it was like an answer to why I got into healthcare in the first place. I was always interested in learning why African Americans lead in most health care related illnesses and diseases.

This information blew me away, because I had drawn the same conclusions. We were taught in slavery days to suck it up and move on. You might think how would you know or how did you reach this conclusion? Well, think about how we were treated back then. For example, a woman could be beaten, have her baby the same day, and be required to go back out in that field picking cotton the very next day.

We all know that having babies back then could kill you, and still kill many women today. This also meant if they got sick they didn't have time to deal with it, but had to keep moving. But what this means today is that we were not allowed to properly process our emotions. We were forced to hold it in. There was a saying when we were younger, "What happens in this house, stays in this house!" So in other words, you would face hell at home, and you better not tell anyone about it. Sadly, many children are living with such ugly scars and stinky mess because in our communities we just didn't talk about it or deal with it.

Unfortunately, this type of behavior and mental state is killing us. If you look at the picture below, it gives you a realistic idea of how emotions impact your health. Look at how each stressor impacts your body and in what areas. Then think about what you do when these stressors occur, so as a result you try to eat, drink, smoke, etc., your problems, hurt, and stress away when these are not the proper solutions to your problem. But facing these problems head on, no matter how they hurt, allows God to heal you.

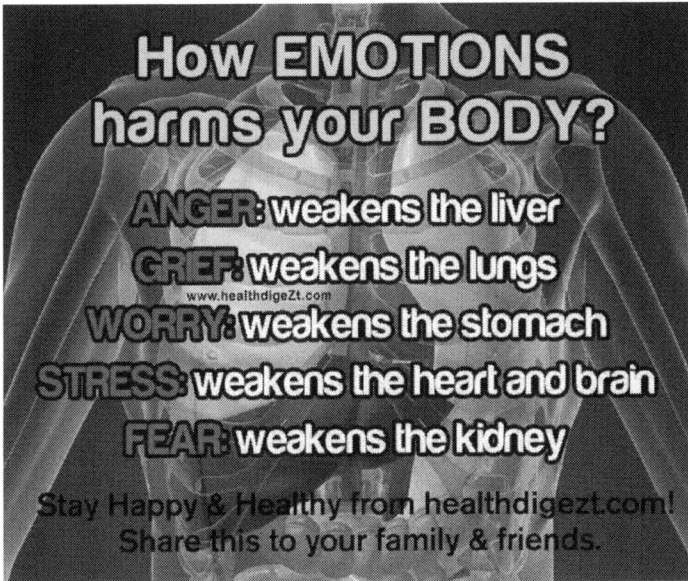

How EMOTIONS harms your BODY?

ANGER: weakens the liver
GRIEF: weakens the lungs
www.healthdigeZt.com
WORRY: weakens the stomach
STRESS: weakens the heart and brain
FEAR: weakens the kidney

Stay Happy & Healthy from healthdigezt.com!
Share this to your family & friends.

I was working with my daughter in February of 2016 in the healing of her ankle sprain injury. Her therapeutic boot had just been removed, and I was trying to assist her. The trainers were working with her at school, but I was also working with her at home. So she advised me of her pain and distress with each time she turned her ankle a certain way or had to put pressure on the ball of her foot. So I began this little saying, "You got to hurt to heal!" It became a chant for me, and she realized, okay, in order for me to get better and this ankle to heal, I am going to have to put some pressure on it. I am going to have to do some exercises to make it stronger, and in that process I am going to have to hurt to heal.

It was as if an alarm went off in my head, and God began to speak to me in that moment. After the filing of the divorce, I wanted to get the girls counseling to make sure they would be okay. So I spoke to a counselor who asked me, "Have you grieved?" I thought, I am concerned about them, so what does this have to do with me?

She said, "If you don't know how to grieve, how will they?"

This question weighed on me for months. God showed me through this book, speaking and writing I would be forced to come face to face and grieve some of my biggest hurts to get the healing that I needed.

I was thinking, God, I have been running this marathon called life. If I stopped for a moment to grieve things in my childhood, in my teen years, having my first child, the marriage, the divorce, etc., I am not sure I would be able to stand up!

But in all reality that wasn't the case. I started doing my research on grieving and mourning, and I was surprised at what I learned. Here is a little information from the WebMD website that I was able to find. Look at how emotions impact your health and think of how anger, fear, stress, worrying, etc., can impact your health over time. I was surprised to see how many of those emotions are connected to grief and mourning.

Grief
Grief is a natural response to loss. It's the emotional suffering you feel when something or someone you love is taken away. The more significant the loss, the

more intense the grief will be. We typically associate grief with death but it is associated to any loss which includes:

- Divorce or relationship breakup
- Loss of health
- Losing a job
- Loss of financial stability
- A miscarriage
- Retirement
- Death of a loved one or pet
- Loss of a cherished dream
- A loved one's serious illness
- Loss of a friendship
- Loss of safety after a trauma
- Selling the family home

Here is a list of the stages of grief:

Denial, numbness, and shock: This stage serves to protect the individual from experiencing the intensity of the loss. Numbness is a normal reaction to an immediate loss and should not be confused with "lack of caring." As the individual slowly acknowledges the impact of the loss, denial and disbelief will diminish.

Bargaining: This stage may involve persistent thoughts about what could have been done to prevent the loss. People can become preoccupied about ways that things could have been better. If this stage is not properly resolved, intense feelings of remorse or guilt may interfere with the healing process.

Depression: This stage of grief occurs in some people after they realize the true extent of the loss. Signs of depression may include sleep and appetite disturbances, a lack of energy and concentration, and crying spells. A person may feel loneliness, emptiness, isolation, and self-pity.

Anger: This reaction usually occurs when an individual feels helpless and powerless. Anger can stem from a feeling of abandonment through a loved one's death. An individual may be angry at a higher power or toward life in general.

Acceptance: In time, an individual may be able to come to terms with various feelings and accept the fact that the loss has occurred. Healing can began once the loss becomes integrated into the individual's set of life experiences.

God wants you to trust him with your hurts so that he can truly provide healing. Our pastor shared a different perspective to Jesus raising Lazarus from the dead. Jesus told Lazarus' family to show him where he lay, and then instructed them to move the stone from his grave.

Jesus didn't need them to tell him where Lazarus lay or to move the stone. The significance is in him telling them to do it. He reminded us how bad his body might have smelled at day four of being buried as rigor mortis set in. He said that just like in that story, God already knows about all our hurts and pains. But we are killing ourselves suppressing it and not dealing with it. I feel that until we take our hurts to our father in exchange for our healing, we are killing ourselves internally.

Reliving some of these hurts had me in tears at one point and laughing the next, but if hurting to get my healing is necessary then I would rather hurt and get over it. The problem is that we don't trust God enough to bring him our hurts and share our stories to help other people. You may hear people saying that is too much, and we shouldn't be talking about this or that. But then I look around at the state of our world. The devil is waging war, and we are still quiet. All hurt isn't bad. If you have given birth, then you have dealt with contractions. If you have been injured and had to rehab back to health, then you know about this hurt to healing. When I was in the Army, I saw soldiers and people hurting. I saw people coming back from war to protect and serve this country who were out their right mind with PTSD. So I encourage you to take your hurts to God and allow yourself the proper time and the process to grieve that loss so that you can be healed.

I am thankful that I was required to go through this process so that God could provide healing.

15

Amazing: To God Be all the Glory

"Until you can praise and thank God for the good, the bad and the ugly, you are simply living, not thriving."

As I close this chapter in my life and move forward with what God has in store for me, I am still amazed at how amazing God is.

Philippians 3:14
I press on toward the goal to win the prize for which God has called me heavenward in Christ Jesus.

I back over my life and see all that I thought I had survived. God was trying to tell me, "Tiffany, these are things you have overcome. You have to know that there is a difference in surviving something and overcoming it." See below.

O·ver·come

- Succeed in dealing with (a problem or difficulty).
- get the better of, prevail over, control, get/bring under control, master, conquer, defeat, beat;
- get over, get a grip on, curb, subdue;
- Defeat (an opponent); prevail.

Survive

- Continue to live or exist, especially in spite of danger or hardship.
- Continue to live or exist in spite of (an accident or ordeal).
- Remain alive after the death of (a particular person).

God showed me that some people have survived things while others have overcome them. I have been blessed as I wrote this book. As mentioned, I started writing this book while I was a young girl in a dark place. Life had dealt me a blow that would take me most of my life to comprehend. Many years later, in God's timing, when I was in a place and at a place to truly receive this understanding, he provided it.

So many years I have spent my life cold-hearted, angry and mad at the world. Foolishly, I had given the devil the victory for that many years. But God showed me he loved me and that he kept me in my right mind. He showed me that he was there the entire time. He told me, "I loved you no less than I did when I watched them brutally beat my only son for you and others before you were even a thought."

I hope you realize if you focus on him, he will do amazingly above all you could ever want or ask. I struggled in some chapters, I cried at some points, couldn't even continue writing at another point. But the glory is all God's. I forgave my mom many years ago. and I am amazed at the beautiful woman of God she has become. I am amazed at how she can still laugh, smile and praise God in the midst of her hurts and trials.

I am amazed that I still love, forgive, smile, laugh and pray for the loved ones that caused me a lot of hurts and pains. I forgive, I love, and most importantly when I completed this book, I became an overcomer. I urge you to seek God's face and to be obedient to him. I pray that you realize that God loves you, even when it doesn't look or feel good. He loves us when it's bad and ugly. He loves us when it's good. I can boldly stand and say I give him all the glory for my life.

I pray that as you bring this book to a close, you will find the courage to look back over your life. Re-evaluate some things and realize until you are delivered and healed from some of those deep hurts, you will never truly thrive as you may desire. I don't care if you have to start one at a time and list them on a sticky note or a note card. But take your hurts to him and allow him to provide healing that you desperately need. In the process of writing this book, I have lost a lot of friends and loved ones along the way. I understand that some people come in your life for a season and others for a lifetime.

I pray for kids that are still hurting or being hurt. I pray for adults who are still suffering from hurts that occurred in their childhood. People ask, "Why are you so forgiving?" I can only explain that I ask God for forgiveness daily.

But forgiveness is also for you as well as for them. So the longer you hold unforgiveness, bitterness and anger in your heart, you are only harming yourself. Someone once said, "Unforgiveness is like allowing someone to live rent free in your heart!" Sad but true; the work, stress and anger you put in to remind someone constantly that they hurt you is mind-blowing. Maybe in this book you will see if I can love, forgive and be healed, so can you.

Notes

Chapter 7
The Free On-line Dictionary of Computing, © Denis
Howe 2010 http://foldoc.org pg. 57

Chapter 14
The Free On-line Dictionary of Computing, © Denis
Howe 2010 http://foldoc.org pg. 122

McGolderick M, Walsh F (2011). Death, loss, and the
family life cycle. In M. McGoldrick et al., eds., The
Expanded Family Life Cycle: Individual, Family, and
Social Perspectives, 4th ed. Boston: Allyn and Bacon.

Newman BM, Newman PR (2012). Understanding
death, dying, and bereavement. In Development
Through Life: A Psychosocial Approach, 11th ed., pp.
601-623. Belmont, CA: Wadsworth Cengage Learning.

Smith M.A., Segal, Jeanne, Ph. D. (2016) Coping with
Grief and Loss Understanding the Grieving Process
Retrieved from:
http://www.helpguide.org/articles/grief-loss/coping-
with-grief-and-loss.htm

WebMD Medical Reference from Healthwise. (2016)
Coping With Grief

Retrieved from; http://www.webmd.com/mental-health/mental-health-coping-with-grief

WebMD Medical Reference from Healthwise. (2016) Grief and Grieving - Topic Overview Retrieved from; http://www.webmd.com/balance/tc/grief-and-grieving-topic-overview

Chapter 15
The Free On-line Dictionary of Computing, © Denis Howe 2010 http://foldoc.org pg. 127

Author Biography
and Personal Message

Tiffany Anderson, also known as Oneofakind Tiffany, is a native of Oklahoma, where she spent her entire childhood. She is now a motivational speaker and author, and the dedicated and hard working mother of two beautiful daughters, Jia Taylor – the Gift – and Tiana Dai – the wise one.

She is a US Army Veteran with a Bachelor's of Science in Healthcare Administration / Management. Currently, she is enrolled at University of Phoenix for a double Master's in Business and Healthcare Administration and Management. Tiffany selected Healthcare Administration and Management as a career path because she wanted to be a greater asset to her family, community and children. Studying our past, present and current health system has provided Tiffany with greater insight into our health system. She has been sharing this wealth of information on her job, in her mentor group, and within her own home

Tiffany is the founder of Oneofakind Girls, a mentor group in Dallas through which she demonstrates her passion for helping and inspiring and empowering all girls. Her motto is simply to empower, inspire and equip young girls to be all God created them to be. She was awarded the Spirit of Service Award in December

2015 from University of Phoenix. In early 2016, she was awarded the Presidential Service Lifetime Achievement award from President Barack Obama for her continued years of service in Girl Scouts and as her daughter's Girl Scout leader as a Juliette for two years, service to her community, through church and countless other volunteer service opportunities. Tiffany has consistently been dedicated to serving and helping others for nearly twenty years and counting.

Tiffany says: In this book, I share how I have been hurt a greater part of my life, and as crazy as it sounds, it would be much later in life I would learn that it was all preparation for my destiny. I'm still hurting even as I put my feelings into this book to help someone else. I'm hurting for the little girl who had nothing to live for, but more importantly hurting for those who are experiencing these things even today. We have to be more accountable to our loved ones in our homes and communities. Stop pretending that we don't know abuse is taking place, whether it is physical or sexual. Abuse plagues us in the forms of sexual molestation, rape – which often results in cervical cancer – and other generational curses. If you love someone, hold them accountable. If you know that a loved one is being hurt, help them. If you don't help them, their past can haunt and hinder them forever. God has shown me that things I have overcome in my life have no limits and boundaries because it is all for his glory. I hope to continue to assist our young girls, but also to share a part of my life that somehow brings hope, love, forgiveness and the message of God's love to anyone who will listen.

.

Made in the USA
Columbia, SC
29 September 2024